SEVEN ROLES

HOW TO BE MORE...YOU

DR. NANCY MCCONLOGUE

Copyright © 2025 by Dr. Nancy A. McConlogue

All rights reserved. No portion of this book may be reproduced, stored, or transmitted in any form without written permission from the author, except as permitted by U.S. copyright law.

This book is intended for informational and educational purposes only. The Seven Roles framework provides insights into mindset and decision-making but does not constitute financial, legal, career, or psychological advice. Readers are responsible for their own decisions and should consult appropriate professionals when making choices that impact their personal, financial, or professional lives. Neither the author nor publisher shall be liable for any outcomes resulting from the use of this material.

1st edition 2025

❦ Formatted with Vellum

DEDICATION

7 7 7 7 7 7 7

To those who are open—

to seeing possibility and a better future,

to creating calm in the middle of chaos,

to sparking energy and moving things forward,

to turning ideas into something real,

to building trust and bringing people together,

to protecting what matters and investing in what lasts,

to thinking clearly, understanding deeply, and asking better questions.

This book is for you.

FOREWORD

WHAT SHE WON'T SAY (WRITTEN BY PKEM)

You might have found this book because you know and respect Dr. Nancy McConlogue's work, are or were a client of hers, heard Google uses this framework for their teams, or maybe you stumbled upon it. Regardless, we want to offer a brief rationale for why you might want to take this seriously.

For us, Dr. Nancy is Mom. If you know Dr. Nancy already, yes, we know we are extremely lucky; if you are just learning of her from this book, we are so happy you get to know a snippet of her as well.

We want to take a moment to explain, from our view, a bit of where this book came from, why it has been impactful for us, and how it might be for you.

Dr. Nancy has been helping people for as long as we can remember. From the time we learned to tie our shoes, she was explaining complex challenges she was helping people solve in therapy. She would keep all details private and ask for opinions, offering wisdom along the way. She has a lifetime of hours invested in work helping individuals, couples, teams, and organizations with life's toughest challenges. Thousands of pairs of eyes looking for input and trusting her with the real hard work—the challenges that keep you up at night, threaten your confidence, disrupt your relationships, or jumble your world. She's always taken a genuine interest in understanding and helping people.

Before the Seven Roles were scientifically validated, founded into a company, and rolled out in corporate settings, they were taped up to our living room wall in our teens. Friends would come over and try to see 'who they were.' We would sit around for hours talking about the nuances and complexities of each of the roles, what caused conflict between roles, and when they were over- or underused. Growing up with the roles helped us not only understand ourselves but also gave us an increased curiosity and appreciation for people.

But this isn't enough of a reason for this book to be worth it to you. Plenty of people love people. Plenty of people help people. You should care about this book because it works. We watched our mom learn and activate the Seven Roles in her own life for the past 20+ years. She's 'played' them all, and while she has favorites, she can pivot between them to reach anyone and solve life's complexities.

As early as we can remember, she's led with the Team Builder Role (you'll learn what you lead with and what might be less comfortable). Conversations with Mom have always been safe and genuine, and her words touch our hearts. Anyone who knows Dr. Nancy personally is smiling reading that sentence.

From young years, we have many memories of Mom's love for learning (Conceptualizer!). Mom's office used to be in a pantry. When that door was closed, it was not a good time to grab a snack. She was getting her master's while homeschooling four kids ages 6-12 while working as a marriage and family therapist. A busy lady that didn't mind a lot of books.

As long as we remember, she's also brought in that Implementor Role. Mom's been nonstop, overbooked, overworked, and determined to say yes to any need. She used to wake up at 4 AM, and often still does, because that's the only time when the tasks of the world don't dominate her time. You'll see through this book the culmination of her Conceptualizer skills. Her ability to take thoroughness to a level unmatched by any, along with her love of research and clarity, is the unseen driver of her excellence. She is the most well-read and researched individual we know, but she'll never flaunt or admit to it.

Then there's the Investor Role. She treasured all the things she owned. Boxes for shoes were saved; items were treated with respect, and gifts meant a great deal—both given and received. She sees value opportunities in projects and people and is intentional about where her time goes. She is also the master negotiator, making sure that in every dispute or conflict, you knew she was searching or mediating for a win-win.

While we've always known her to play these four roles, we've been able to witness her develop the remaining three.

In high school and during our engagements with Google, Dr. Nancy played more of the Luminary Role (begrudgingly, though only we knew that!). She sat on the school board, invited families over every weekend, and tired herself out throwing massive birthday parties for us. We always had people over. We saw it wear on her, though. Some people would overstay their welcome, and it was hard for her to set boundaries while also being super fun. That is to say, her understanding of the roles comes from practicing out the shortcomings of a role and learning when she over- or underuses a role.

Experiencing her develop the Organizer Role in our teens wasn't the most welcome. Rules, rules, rules! Home by a certain time, pants a certain length, and abiding by authority. All good things, and thankfully her Team Builder skills were still there while she played these!

Prophet is probably her weakest role (sorry, Mom), but I think the reason she and my Dad work so well together is that Prophet is his strongest. They complemented each other and pushed each other to stretch in the ways that were least comfortable. For the Prophet Role, life does not require her to step into it often, but she can when necessary. We have seen it most clearly in the picturesque 'mama bear' mode whenever someone wronged one of her kids or if a telephone provider called one too many times.

This is what's amazing about the roles: some of them fatigue us while they bring life to others; some of them are easy for us and absolutely unimaginable for others. People have beautiful fingerprints, and the roles give us a language to appreciate others and stretch ourselves.

While we're sure Dr. Nancy has many hopes and dreams for this book, we believe more than anything, she wants you to be curious about yourself and not limited by anything in the direction of your endeavors. There could be a mended relationship, a surge of confidence, a plan for your next step, a strengthened team, increased happiness, or a new grand idea from the activation of this book.

This book is for every person, every role. As you explore its content, you'll see how each aspect reflects the Seven Roles:

- Every story is a real person with whom she has walked life (Team Builder).
- Every word is carefully chosen (Conceptualizer).
- It is written to empower you to take charge of your growth (Organizer).
- She gives it to you straight (Prophet).
- She provides you with tangible next steps (Implementor).
- She tells you growth ideas in a way you can be excited about (Luminary).
- And she has made this to be worth your time (Investor).

This is for those who want to grow.

We hope this gave you, even if small, a snapshot of the woman we're honored to call our mom.

Patrick, Kevan, Erin & Meaghan

*In every moment, we wear the role that shapes our future.
The power lies not in the role itself, but in our ability to choose it.
Dr. Nancy McConlogue*

CONTENTS

Seven Reasons You Will Love The Seven Roles	15
Introduction	17
Unit 1: How We Role	20
Roles = Change	
Unit II: The Seven Roles Framework	37
POLITIC	
Unit III: The Seven Roles	58
Your Role Your Choice	
Envisioning the Prophet Role	60
Living as a Visionary	
Planning the Organizer Role	90
Living Organized	
Living Out the Luminary Role	125
Living Outloud	
Appreciating the Investor Role	149
Living Substantially	
Trusting the Team Builder Role	182
Living Kindly	
Executing the Implementor Role	217
Living To Do	
Thinking Like the Conceptualizer Role	252
Living Thoughtfully	
Unit IV: Putting the Roles to Work for You	280
For the Role Masters	
Role Pairing	281
Mixing and Matching the Roles	
Unit V: The End or is it The Beginning?	298
Onward!	
Quick Quiz	301
Your Role'dex	305
For the Conceptualizer	309
Credits	313
Acknowledgments	315
About the Author	319

SEVEN REASONS YOU WILL LOVE THE SEVEN ROLES

1. You get to learn something new.
2. You get a simple roadmap to be more…you.
3. It is proven. It is based on results from thousands of people across many trainings.
4. It is easy to remember and easy to apply.
5. It offers real tools for better communication.
6. For those who like to know more about everything, it offers layers upon layers of different uses.
7. It is fun. It's a great conversation starter.

WHAT ARE YOUR TOP ROLES?

INTRODUCTION

Do you ever wish you could be more? To be different than who you are? Or maybe not to be someone different but to be able to act differently?

- To boldly challenge the status quo, and shape what's next
- To be that organized person who always has a plan—and never loses their keys
- To be a wise investor of both your money and your time
- To step into a room and inspire others with your inspirational energy and enthusiasm
- To be the smart one, the one who knows the answers and makes well thought out decisions
- To share genuine compassion, connecting with others in ways that builds lasting trust
- Or to be the one who, frankly, just feels good about the day in front of you, excited to get to get started on your to-do list

This book is about playing seven specific roles that can support you to be any or all of these people. It is a helping tool for being more; more confident, more caring, more engaged, more productive, more thoughtful, more persuasive and more valuable. This likely sounds too good to be true but before you toss out the idea, what if what you need to change is a few acting instructions? A helpful script to follow?

Sometimes all we need to know in order to step into new behaviors is to learn how a desired role thinks and acts. And then it's simply a choice to practice the behaviors that stretch you from who you are into more of who you are. The goal is not to be someone you aren't, the goal is to be more… you. This book is a guide to the Seven Roles that have helped so many achieve their big daring goals. And it can help you too.

First, you will want to identify the roles you already play well.

Then you will want to learn about the roles you don't use as often or as well and choose which ones you want to practice.

Finally, when you know all Seven Roles and the purpose and behaviors of each, you move into advanced role play. The ultimate goal is to learn to use the right role at the right time and most importantly, with the right people. You will still be you but you will have new skills and responses and insights and perspectives that can help you be more.

My hope is that you find the Seven Roles valuable in meeting your daily goals, your normal life and your everyday relationships. But, even better, my big outrageous life dream is that the Seven Roles will help you fulfill your big outrageous life dreams.

Big dreams take all Seven Roles. Big dreams take all of you.

This brings us back to the core idea of this book. The Seven Roles offer perspectives and strategies to help you grow—deepening and strengthening the roles you already play—and, more importantly, to help you change, by adopting and mastering new roles altogether.

Growth is about taking who you already are and making it stronger. Change is about stepping into roles you've never fully embraced before. Both require courage, openness, and practice. It isn't always easy, but it's always doable—and always worth it.

Learn about the Seven Roles. Learn about your own roles. And then grow them all. Your stronger roles and your weaker roles can all be strengthened. Read on to learn why. And how.

"The first step towards getting somewhere is to decide you're not going to stay where you are." -J.P. Morgan.

UNIT 1: HOW WE ROLE
ROLES = CHANGE

Chapter Overview

Roles are a powerful tool for change, but they are not a widely known framework. You could skip this chapter and jump straight to the information about the Seven Roles, but sometimes understanding the why behind the what provides a structure—a way to organize and make sense of new information.

Since the Seven Roles may be unfamiliar at first, this chapter lays the foundation, giving you a mental framework to see where roles fit.

The first step in mastering role play is understanding what roles are—and what they aren't. We'll begin by comparing roles and personalities, two very different concepts. In a nutshell, personality is about consistency, but that's not the message of roles. With roles, change is your choice.

Next, we'll explore the brain's remarkable capacity for change, its cognitive flexibility with all the benefits—including enhanced creativity, learning, resilience, and stress management. By the end of this section, hopefully, you'll see that change isn't just good—it's possible, within your control, and quite frequently, necessary.

Finally, you'll find discussion questions to help you apply what you've learned, plus a quick tip to get you started right away.

ROLES, ROLES & MORE ROLES

We all play roles. Whether it's at work, in our personal lives, or within our communities, we have to adapt to diverse and fluid scenarios, wearing different hats to achieve different goals. But do you stop to think about the roles you are choosing? It is more likely that the roles you play every day are practiced habits with automatic and rote responses to various scenarios. You play so many different roles every day without thinking about them at all.

For example, suppose you are working out at the gym. The role you are playing there does not include enthusiastically and loudly explaining to everyone around you how to get the most out of the equipment they are using. However, if you are the instructor in a spin class at that same gym, that is exactly the role  you play. In that case, being vocal and instructive and encouraging and even challenging and critiquing is exactly the role that is needed.

We all play roles and we play them all the time. Different roles are adopted to achieve different goals.

This book is about seven very specific roles that work together to achieve big goals. You play some of them brilliantly, and some of them maybe not as well. My goal is to offer information you can use to understand, strengthen, and then choose when and what roles to play.

Let's begin at the beginning and talk about what a role is and what a role isn't.

WHAT IS A ROLE?

Roles are rules for how to act. They are expectations, responsibilities, and behaviors that we choose to adopt and follow or not. Roles are found in every aspect of life, from our personal relationships to our professional careers. They are the building blocks of social structure. They help us to navigate the  complex web of relationships and interactions that make up the world around us.

In many cases, roles are formalized and well-defined. In the workplace, for example, there may be clearly defined roles such as manager, supervisor, or entry-level employee. If you can imagine a title, you are likely imagining a role. A coach, a teacher, a student, a player, a partner, a volunteer, a parent, a child: all are examples of roles that have some common set of expectations, behaviors, activities, or attributes.

In other situations, roles may be more fluid and open-ended and remain unlabeled. For example, in a group of friends there may be the informal leader who tends to organize events or another who plays the part of the group spokesperson. These roles might ebb and flow based on the people, the activity or the environment.

Roles are highly context-dependent. They are likely to change over time as circumstances evolve. For example, a parent's role develops as their child grows, or a person's role within a company may change as they gain new skills and take on new responsibilities or as the needs of the company change. While we might appreciate the value of consistency, life seems to offer a steady stream of change.

Why Why and Why?

Why learn about roles at all? Why the Seven Roles? And why does this matter to you?

UNIT 1: HOW WE ROLE

Roles offer a straightforward way to view different perspectives for any task or interaction with others. By thinking in terms of roles, you can imagine and then learn how to act in that role.

For instance, consider a work scenario where you are promoted to a new position. You imagine what that will look like and then learn all you can about your upcoming role as you start practicing. Your approach, your behaviors, and even your attitude changes as you change roles.

As mentioned in the previous section, we all play roles constantly. Any title, such as parent, leader, friend, employee, runner, or volunteer, represents a role. These roles shift and change over time, with different activities and across different relationships.

Most importantly, how you play a role is entirely your choice, making the idea of roles synonymous with adaptability. Life happens to you. You choose your response. Role play—the way you engage with and shift between roles—is a choice 100% of the time.

Tornado Roles

Recently, at a beautiful restaurant in Tennessee, a tornado warning interrupted the smoothly running dinner service. For those who don't know the tornado warning system, there are different levels of alerts. A tornado watch means that conditions are right for a tornado to form. A tornado warning is more serious and means that a tornado has touched down. The warning drew the staff and customers to news outlets to determine how near the touchdown was to the restaurant. It was decided that it was near enough to seek cover.

The entire restaurant was evacuated to the basement shelter amidst confusion as the standard rules of action in the restaurant were interrupted. The roles had shifted from restaurant rules to a new set of rules where the staff and guests intermingled, operating as one big basement team. Those who had more leadership qualities led the way to the basement with authority as though they had been intentionally selected for the position. Those who were planners took supplies with them (which caused some jealousy during the long waiting period). Those who were security minded assessed the environment, checking on status updates and reviewing the tornado path. Those who were more service minded assisted those who were having trouble with it all. There was those who relished the excitement of it all, hovering near the door hoping to catch a glimpse of a tornado while others stayed as far away as possible repeatedly insisting the door should be and remain firmly closed. And then there were the networkers, who thought this was simply the best time to meet new people. Everyone intermingled, the staff and the guests, all playing very different roles from those in the restaurant only a few minutes earlier.

After the tornado had passed, the entire group immediately returned to the standard rules of action and the conversations and behaviors that had drawn them together during the emergency, were halted. And most remarkably, this was done with only one sentence, "The tornado warning has passed." It was simply understood that now restaurant rules of action were back in play and everyone almost instantly followed them.

Roles follow rules of action whether or not they are overtly stated. You may find that some roles are very easy to deliver and some are simply not 'how you are made'. Are you the networker? The one who brings supplies? The one who hopes to catch a glimpse of a tornado? Personality and role play interact as we encounter life, role play opportunities, and explains why some people stood by the door hoping to catch a glimpse of a tornado and others wanted the door barricaded. Our personalities will help and even encourage us to perform some roles and be less helpful when performing others. But anyone can choose to overcome their natural tendency and move toward the door to see the action or decide to play it safe and move away. We have a choice in playing roles that is influenced by our personality but not determined by it.

Also, notice that those same personality types that were demonstrated during the tornado, went back to their expected roles. In other words, while my personality might desire to engage and network and socialize, my job might be to clear the table so that is the role I play. It is not what my personality would like to do, but it is my role if I expect to be paid. We all play roles that we need to play, whether or not they align perfectly with our personalities.

Why These Seven Roles?

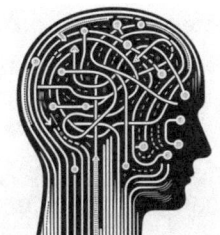

Why focus on the Seven Roles? Because they offer a clear, practical framework for achieving your biggest goals and dreams. Each role represents a crucial function needed to turn vision into reality. By understanding them, you can identify what your goals demand—and where your strengths or blind spots might be holding you back.

If you want to see the roles in action, check out Sarah's story in the next chapter. It illustrates how the Seven Roles work together to drive meaningful progress.

The Seven Roles also provide key insights into when you might need to switch gears—because every major goal and most relationships require all seven at some point. Are you using them all? Discovering which roles you naturally play and which ones you tend to avoid might explain why your progress isn't where you want it to be.

Let's explore three major reasons why understanding and applying the Seven Roles can be a life-changer for you.

First, it can provide your next step. The Seven Roles serve as a roadmap, outlining essential steps to achieve your goals—including ones you might otherwise overlook. If you hit a roadblock, the solution might be as simple as stepping into a less familiar role. Sometimes, our favorite roles can actually hinder progress. By shifting roles, you shift your mindset and behaviors, which directly impacts your results.

Next, the Seven Roles empower you. When you understand that roles are chosen, not fixed, you gain control over your outcomes. Stepping into different roles challenges you to develop new skills and perspectives. Life doesn't just happen to you—you happen to life.

Finally, **understanding the Seven Roles isn't just about you–it's also about the people around you.** Knowing your role strengths is crucial, but it's only half of the puzzle. The other half is recognizing the roles *others* play.

Whether you're navigating a tough conversation at work or deepening your closest relationships, the Seven Roles give you a powerful vocabulary to clearly understand yourself and meaningfully connect with others.

Let's sum it up. Why use the Seven Roles? Because they expand your options—in how you pursue goals, how you adapt to challenges, and how you build stronger relationships.

Roles are NOT personalities

Roles are a choice. Whether at work, at home, at the gym, with family, or out with friends, we naturally adjust our "costumes" and behaviors to align with the expectations of our environment—yet our core personality remains constant.

Personality and role use are not the same. Personality consists of the innate traits you are born with and tend to maintain throughout your life. While research suggests that personality can evolve over time, these changes happen gradually, often over decades. (*50-Year Personality Study*)

In contrast, a role is like a toolkit—a set of behaviors, thoughts, values, and mindsets that we can consciously choose to adopt in the moment.

UNIT 1: HOW WE ROLE 27

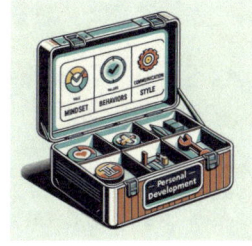

The beauty of roles is that they are changeable. They can be influenced, expanded, and, most importantly, intentionally played or intentionally set aside. Unlike personality, which tends to remain stable, roles are flexible. We hold the reins—we choose which roles we want to play in any given situation.

This is because we hold the reins when it comes to the roles we want to play in any given situation. We can decide to behave in a way that fits a particular role, even if it goes against our natural tendencies or our personality. For instance, if we tend to be more introverted, we can push ourselves to adopt more extraverted behaviors to enhance our communication with others.

When we consciously adopt a role, we push beyond our perceived limitations. In doing so, we discover that we are capable of more than we initially believed. Just as life skills grow with experience, so does the depth of our *roleset*—the ranked list of the Seven Roles that reflects our strengths, tendencies, and areas for growth.

By understanding the different roles and intentionally choosing the ones best suited for a given situation, we not only increase our effectiveness, we actively shape who we become—more adaptable, more capable, and ultimately better prepared for whatever comes next.

"Every time you make a choice you are turning the central part of you... into something a little different than it was before." -C. S. Lewis

---

YOUR NEW FAVORITE WORD

Change is the crux of successful role expansion. As discussed in the previous section, this is not a change in who you are but a change in how you act.

To change a role, there are two very distinct actions that must take place. One is to let go of existing behaviors and values that contradict that role, and the other is to adopt the actions, attitude, and mindset of the new role.

A simple way to picture this is to imagine you are halfway through eating a delicious cookie when you remember you are working yourself away from sugar. At this point, it would be easiest to just finish the cookie. The harder choice and the one you wish you wanted to take would be to put the cookie down and replace it with a glass of water.

Role change requires a similar dedication of focus. You will naturally want to return to the familiar patterns. It is always easier to finish the cookie. It will always be easier to stay with the roles you know.

This leads us to a common objection to any growth strategy. Can I change?

Your Brain is Made for Change

The answer is, of course, a resounding *yes*! In fact, you can't NOT change. You are changing as you read this. As the saying goes, change is the constant. The good news is that we are literally designed to change and develop over the course of a lifetime, constantly acquiring new information from our surroundings and adapting.

Each choice we make has the power to influence the direction of our lives and shape the changes we experience. By consciously making choices that align with our desired outcomes, we can proactively drive personal change. Consider how impactful choices can be when we engage in a new skill, pursue further education, or commit to a healthy lifestyle plan.

Every decision we make, whether big or small, has an impact on whatever is next in our lives. From the moment we wake up in the morning through each task we prioritize in our day, our choices shape not only our current experience but our future as well.

The problem is we often try to avoid change, especially when it comes to ourselves. "*I am who I am*" becomes our mantra. While the world changes like crazy around us, we hold on to the idea that our existing toolset is good enough.

We resist change, or worse, we ignore it. Stepping out of our comfort zones and embracing change requires effort, a willingness to face uncertainty, loss of control (perceived and real) and maybe worst of all, the feeling of ineptness. For this and others reasons, our brains seek familiarity and repeatable patterns, naturally gravitating towards the known and predictable with a behavioral pattern we are familiar with. Changing how you act will certainly be challenging and likely won't be done well at first.

Why put ourselves through that? Why read and apply books like this that challenge how you think, feel, and act? The answer is simple and conclusive. Change is good for your brain. Let's look at that in a bit more detail.

"The only person you are destined to become is the person you decide to be." -Ralph Waldo Emerson

---

Flex Brain Flex!

What happens when we choose to grow with change? The answer lies in the power of the brain's remarkable ability to not only adapt but also to evolve.

When we consciously decide to adopt new behaviors, we stimulate our brain's mental nimbleness, a characteristic known as "cognitive flexibility." Scientific research highlights the many benefits that come with this wonderful mental agility.

Here are a few of the reasons why embracing change and flexing your "cognitive change muscle" is worth the effort.

Cognitive flexibility boosts creativity. People with high cognitive flexibility can often come up with inventive solutions to problems and easily adjust their thinking to navigate complex situations. Simply put, they can think outside the box (Diamond, 2013; Miyake et al., 2000).

Cognitive flexibility helps learning. Higher cognitive flexibility can help improve how we process information, and perform in academics. It helps us understand things from various angles, and different perspectives encouraging retention. It enhances learning (Blair & Razza, 2007; Zelazo et al., 2010).

Cognitive flexibility builds resilience. Cognitive flexibility plays a key role in managing those out-of-control type emotions by enhancing the ability to switch gears. This allows us to better adapt to messy situations and bounce back from tough times. Embracing change builds resilience (Opitz, 2014; Thompson & Waltz, 2007).

Cognitive flexibility improves real communication. Enhanced cognitive flexibility can lead to improved communication, increased empathy, and greater understanding in social interactions. It's like getting a better antenna for picking up and understanding others' signals. It helps us hear better (Katz et al., 2014; Rudebeck et al., 2008).

Cognitive flexibility offers a healthier path to aging. For older adults, heightened cognitive flexibility equates to better mental functioning and a reduced risk of cognitive decline. It's an insurance policy to help keep a sharp mind as you age—invest now for rewards later (Nouchi et al., 2016; Stern, 2009).

Cognitive flexibility improves overall mental health. Overall mental health is positively impacted when you feel more in control of your life choices. People who demonstrate greater cognitive flexibility often feel less anxious, less depressed, and generally better about life. Cognitive flexibility promotes the ability to feel good (DeLorenzo et al., 2018; Moritz et al., 2010).

So, what might this look like in our everyday life? For starters, cognitive flexibility enables us to multitask efficiently—a skill that's certainly in high demand in today's fast-paced world. It allows us to shift our attention swiftly between tasks to rapidly adapt to different environments.

Moreover, cognitive flexibility helps us tackle new situations head-on. As life tosses us curveballs, we can respond nimbly and effectively rather than feeling overwhelmed. Having cognitive flexibility means being more open-minded, resilient, and capable of managing stress when facing new challenges.

Perhaps the most significant advantage of cognitive flexibility is its role in learning from our mistakes. Instead of stubbornly sticking to our ways or blaming our mistakes on unchangeable personality traits, cognitive flexibility allows us to reflect, analyze, and adapt. And just like our muscles, our brains grow stronger when challenged.

Let's look at an example story about Alice who wanted a different future but needed to embrace the discomfort of the unfamiliar. Alice, as you will see, needed to choose change if she wanted to change her life trajectory.

Alice: Change in Action

Alice, a third-year graduate student, struggled with public speaking. She would get extremely nervous and anxious when presenting in front of her class, which caused her to stumble and lose her train of thought. However, she knew that effective speaking skills were an important part of her future career goals.

Alice decided to take action to improve. She enrolled in a public speaking course and joined a speaking club on campus. She also began practicing speeches with others that she trusted, helping her to build confidence.

Through consistent practice, and some amount of stubborn determination, Alice's public speaking skills improved significantly. She became more confident and comfortable in front of an audience, and her presentations became smoother and more engaging. The more she enjoyed it, the more her style became enjoyable to others. This helped her to excel and stand out in job interviews as she approached graduation.

Ironically, she ended up choosing a job in corporate training. She found that her personal victory over her speaking anxiety gave her useful insights into the wider field of growth and personal development. She also found that she actually enjoyed speaking to groups!

Change, which Alice now could personally attest to, is not only possible, it's life changing. This is now the message she wants to share with others.

When you choose to embrace change—like Alice did—you're choosing a healthier brain, more resilience, stronger learning, and an open future.

Say yes to change!

SUMMARY

Congratulations on completing the first chapter of this book and the beginning of your roles journey. Let's recap what we've covered.

We began by defining what a role is. We learned that a role is not the same as a personality but rather a set of behaviors and actions that we choose to adopt to fulfill a particular function or purpose. Roles are found in every aspect of our lives, from personal relationships to professional careers. They help us navigate social structures and interactions.

"Those who cannot change their minds cannot change anything."
-George Bernard Shaw

Moreover, we debunked the misconception that roles are fixed and innate—we have the power to choose the roles we want to play. We learned that roles are flexible and context-dependent, evolving over time along with our circumstances.

We also looked at the concept of change and how relevant it is to every decision we make. Think about it—every decision, no matter how big or small, has consequences. From the moment we wake up in the morning and choose what to wear, to the tasks we prioritize throughout the day, our choices shape our experiences and determine the path we take. The power lies in our ability to consciously make choices that align with our desired outcomes.

Lastly, we talked about the power of cognitive flexibility that comes from learning to embrace change, including enhanced problem-solving, critical thinking, emotional well-being, interpersonal relationships, healthier aging, and stress management.

Throughout this chapter, the Seven Roles framework is presented as a toolkit for growth helping you to manage and even encourage change.

ONE QUICK TIP

This book is an invitation to see the world through seven entirely different lenses. But change doesn't happen by reading alone. It happens when you pause, reflect, and then—write your thoughts down.

Start a fresh notebook and keep it close. Use it to jot down notes, questions, or even just a quick sentence about what struck you. You don't have to write long entries. You just have to pay attention to what you're learning.

The discussion points can help with that. Read them. Journal them. Talk them out with others if you can. They're there to get you thinking —about your habits, your patterns, and the roles you tend to play.

If journaling sounds like a chore, try thinking of it as *noticing on paper*. And what you notice can help you grow.

Growth takes effort. It's worth the effort. First step? A notebook and a pen. See what shows up.

"Great things are not done by impulse, but by a series of small things brought together."— *Vincent van Gogh*

DISCUSSION

These questions are here to spark reflection—not just on what you do, but on how you approach change, growth, and challenge. Journaling your thoughts is a powerful first step, but don't stop there. Sometimes the people around us see things we've missed.

Ask someone who knows you well—someone who truly cares—how they've seen you respond to change. What role do they see you lead with? Where do they see you shine? You might be surprised by what they notice.

Whether you're discussing this with a partner, a friend, a mentor, or a group, stay curious. Listen without defending. Consider their insight as another lens through which to see your strengths—and your next steps.

You don't have to figure this out alone. Growth is personal, but it doesn't have to be solitary.

1. What roles in life do you play? Start by listing all the things that you do. For example: parent, partner, construction worker, budgeter, board member, meal planner, volunteer, artist, reader, gym rat, etc.
2. What are your goals in life right now relative to those roles? How content are you with playing those roles as they are now?
3. Reflect on a time when you were required to take on a new, different role. For example, maybe when you were asked to take on more responsibility, or you moved to a completely new area, or like the story of Alice in this chapter, you had to do learn a new skill in order to accomplish a bigger goal. What was challenging? What was rewarding? How did it turn out?
4. On a scale of 1 to 10, how open are you to change?
5. On a scale of 1 to 10, how open are you to changing?

6. How have you changed over the past 5 years? 10 years? Since childhood?
7. When change hits you unexpectedly, what's your first response—resistance or curiosity?
8. When was the last time you had to "change your mind" about something important? What helped you shift perspectives, and what was the result?
9. Think of a recent challenging situation. How might looking at it from a different angle—or someone else's point of view—have changed your response?
10. Create a specific plan for activating this book toward your goals. For example, commit to reading one chapter a day and writing 1-3 sentences in a journal applying what you learn about yourself or the Seven Roles.
11. What is a goal you are trying to accomplish and how is it going? Or, if you don't have a goal right now, what was the last big goal you pursued and how did it go?

"The greatest discovery of all time is that a person can change his future by merely changing his attitude." -Oprah Winfrey

---

UNIT II: THE SEVEN ROLES FRAMEWORK
POLITIC

CHAPTER Overview

In this section, we will be looking at the Seven Roles framework. Some of you skipped ahead to this chapter (I would have) to see what they are and maybe to decide how they relate to you.

We will start by looking at how the roles have helped others and how they can help you. An example is included of the dramatic impact role awareness can have on a relationship and on a career.

Next in this chapter is an overview of all Seven Roles. It is offered as a quick summary with a few key characteristics for each role. Later chapters explore the roles in depth.

Following this is Sarah's story, an example of a business startup requiring the Seven Roles to complete the launch steps.

Then, you will be ready to identify your top roles and your lesser played or weaker roles. We'll go over several options you can use to get started on this process.

By the end of this section, you'll be armed with the tools you need to embark on your own roles growth journey. But for now, let's get started on understanding the foundation and overview of the Seven Roles.

LIFE WITH SEVEN ROLES

Imagine a life where you have a clear vision of where you are headed, the ability to plan and execute your goals, the power to inspire and motivate others, the strategic mindset to manage time, people, and resources effectively, the knack for building strong relationships and collaborations, the drive to take action and get things done, and the analytical thinking and information you need to solve complex problems. This is the world of the Seven Roles.

Whether you are seeking to better your communication style, upgrade your career trajectory, build fulfilling relationships, enhance your leadership abilities, or just better navigate the complexities of life, the Seven Roles provides a roadmap to help you get there.

HOW DO THE SEVEN ROLES HELP?

Role perspectives can solve problems, but if you are unaware of their influence, your favorite or well used roles can negatively influence and even create problems.

Let me share a simple example from a therapeutic context that shows how influential role choices can be and how knowing this can help promote more meaningful dialogue and mutual understanding.

ROLES & THERAPY

Lou & Ren came in for counseling because they could not end a fight. When they weren't fighting, they actually really liked each other and enjoyed shared activities and time together. But the disagreements always seemed unsolvable and were an increasing source of tension. They shared with me their most recent fight which had taken place over the past weekend.

They were packing the car for a hiking adventure, an activity they both looked forward to and mutually enjoyed. As was typical for them, he was in a hurry to leave to maximize their adventure time while she was wanting extra time to pack everything carefully so that setting up the campsite would be easier. She was a planner. He was a doer.

I shared with them the Seven Roles, the seven ways to look at a task like packing a car and asked them to identify their typical role approach. It was an easy question for them as they play their top roles often, both at home and it turned out, at work too.

After briefly reflecting on the descriptions, she quickly identified her strong Organizer Role. She always had a plan for efficiency, but it took time and a system. He saw that his go-to role was always a "let's get this done now" approach. She was approaching from the Organizer Role, he from the Implementor Role.

Regardless of your personal opinion on who is right in this plan vs progress conflict, either way the car gets packed. The real question to resolve, and it must be resolved before even beginning a project like packing the car, is to jointly agree on whose role is leading the task. When they considered this input, it was as if they had been given a key that unlocked the troublesome pattern of their fights.

We spent most of the remainder of the hour dissecting a pile of past fights through the lens provided by the roles. They agreed to learn each other's role approach, or at the very least, learn to appreciate it. They determined that many of their conflicts could have been avoided by simply deferring to the other's preferred role style based on the needs of the task at hand. They also wondered if their lesser played roles could be useful. With that, their role journey had officially begun.

This couple checked in from time to time with questions on their lesser played roles. They began using the roles beyond their personal relationship. The roles they played adjusted as they changed jobs and addressed work issues. I still hear from them now and then and it always includes an encouragement to me to share the roles with others, as it was for them the single most impactful tool they had ever learned.

I have seen so many of this type of *aha* moment with the roles. A few of those stories are scattered throughout this book as examples, with their names changed, of course. People can experience almost instant growth when they realize how differently they look at the world compared to others, especially when they see the value of that different perspective.

There is also relief and a certain amount of pride as the strong roles became strengths to be proud of and the weaker roles became achievable growth opportunities. The idea that you can put on a different mindset often makes it possible to put on that mindset.

Sometimes all we need to change our behavior is to know what other options we have to choose from.

Using the Roles at Work

Originally, I used the Seven Roles with individuals and families, one at a time. We would work together and figure out their role preferences by questioning and conversation. This is the most effective way to discover role strengths but it is very slow.

In order to share the idea and the use of the roles with a wider population, the Seven Roles as a framework needed to be identified and proved. I spent more than ten years investing in learning what was needed to formally validate them. This study culminated in my doctoral work, which confirmed their measurable presence and more

UNIT II: THE SEVEN ROLES FRAMEWORK

importantly, the distinctiveness of the Seven Roles across a diverse demographic. The Seven Team Roles Scale (STRS) was official.

With its validation, its application in the corporate arena became immediately more impactful. It was time to take the Seven Roles to work. Clients could now take the scale both individually and as a team. Individual scores could be mapped alongside team scores.

In 2020, our daughter Erin started Lumiere Sciences, a business that includes training in the Seven Roles. Her business grew and her sister, Meaghan, her sister's husband, Kevin, and her brothers, Kevan and Patrick, all contributed along the way.

The company began offering ten-week roles training courses focused on enhancing team communication and cohesion. Subsequent training was customized, aligning corporate objectives with the collective roles of the audience. This led to live events covering many aspects of corporate dynamics: from bolstering team unity, boosting leadership tactics, facilitating RTO planning, addressing burnout, improving negotiation tactics and upgrading the work from home experience with community building tools and practice. The results were impactful.

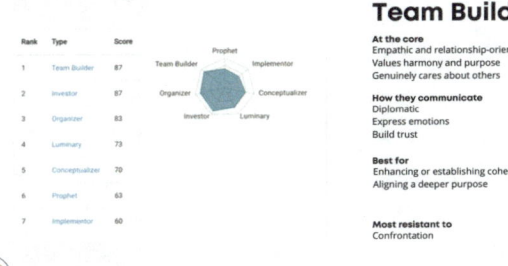

For example, if a company was trying to build team connection and trust, the Team Builder Role was emphasized. Role education and activities were combined to offer team members the methods to practice the tenants of the role.

Or, if the company was focused on growth, efficiency or clarity, the Organizer or Implementor Roles would be highlighted. Likewise, if the value added, profitability, and the importance of viable networks was the focus, the Investor Role became the practice focus.

The biggest surprise emerged in the overall results, revealing a clear and consistent trend: organizations exhibit preferences towards specific rolesets*. These preferences are evident within individual departments, across leadership tiers, and, most surprisingly, throughout the entire organization.

For example, one Fortune 500 company tested high in Team Builder while another similarly sized company tested consistently low in this role, instead showing instead a high affinity for the Conceptualizer Role. This suggests that the very ethos of a company influences or intentionally selects individuals based on expected frequency of a particular role play.

The idea here is profound: if you are in an environment that does not value your top roles, you can choose to be a unique asset to the company by bringing an underrepresented skill or adapt and learn the other roles that are favored. Either solution can work but knowing that you make the choice is far more empowering and likely more effective.

Also, it became measurably obvious that when you are looking for lateral or upward job movement, you should determine what roleset is a best fit for that position and learn those skills. Rolesets change dramatically and consistently the higher up the corporate ladder you

---

* A roleset is a current, ranked, ordered list of the Seven Roles.

are. If your goal is career advancement, practicing the roles used by the position you are aiming for is a good way to prepare.

The scale itself has undergone refinements and expansions since first published. Different versions are now offered that explore role specificities in areas like hiring, leadership, performance reviews, and relationship interplay. The findings continued to validate the robustness and reliability of the STRS, the Seven Team Roles Scale.

The large and growing client base has demonstrated the effectiveness of the Seven Roles as a framework for growth. As individuals and teams understand the Seven Roles, they can choose the roles that align with their goals, their team's goals and their company's goals.

Today, the Seven Roles scale has been used by thousands in diverse settings across many fields including Google, Slack, Meta, and Amazon, as well as startups and mom & pop shops.

The Seven Roles began as a helping tool for clients, then morphed into a corporate tool to help hundreds of teams. Now it returns to its original calling—as a helping tool for you. Onward!

"The journey of a thousand miles begins with one step." -Lao Tzu

THE SEVEN ROLES

This section offers an overview of the Seven Roles to help you get a big picture of all the roles. Each chapter that follows in this book describes the Seven Roles in detail including methods for practicing.

I strongly encourage you to read the chapters in whatever order most interests you. Some people are naturally curious about their strongest or most frequently played roles, while others prefer to explore their weaker or less familiar roles first. Either way works. The chapters are designed to be read in any sequence—each one is completely stand-alone.

That being said, they are presented here in the order of a handy and curiously applicable acronym that spells *POLITIC*: *P*rophet, *O*rganizer, *L*uminary, *I*nvestor, *T*eam Builder, *I*mplementor and *C*onceptualizer.

When you think of role politics, you can imagine a system where all Seven Roles work together in perfect unity toward an intended and beneficial goal.

Of course, I am aware that politics might not be the most positive word today, but maybe the Seven Roles can redeem it, encouraging us to constructively work together.

The Seven Roles in POLITIC order

Prophet: The Visionary who sees the bigger picture and creates a clear vision of the future.

Organizer: The Planner who develops strategies and systems to execute goals efficiently.

Luminary: The Inspirer who motivates and engages others, networks easily, and generates energy and enthusiasm.

Investor: The Strategist who manages resources, evaluates options, and makes decisions that result in optimal outcomes.

Team Builder: The Connector who fosters collaboration based on trust.

Implementor: The Doer who takes action, executes plans, and ensures tasks are completed.

Conceptualizer: The Thinker who analyzes information, seeks knowledge, and shares insights that drive deeper understanding.

"Change the way you look at things and the things you look at change."— Wayne Dyer

---

Now that you know what the Seven Roles are, you might be wondering: how do they actually work together?

The next section offers a real-world example to show the full power of the roles in motion; working together to support a big, outrageous, life dream.

Using the Roles for a Big Outrageous Life Dream

Let's put the roles to work on a life dream and see how they all contribute to the success of the new business.

Sarah is a 30 something, engaging and motivated individual who aspires to start her own sustainable clothing brand. Let's see how each of the Seven Roles comes into play in her entrepreneurial journey.

Sarah: Ethical Fashion Business Startup with the Seven Roles

Sarah loves all things fashion. After graduating from Savannah College of Art and Design, Sarah eagerly started her new career in New York with a company specializing in "fast fashion." However, her excitement was soon overshadowed by a troubling realization she had about the unsustainable practices of the industry.

Prophet Role: Seeing the Future

Disillusioned, Sarah began to inwardly critique the industry she once admired. The waste, the incessant consumerism, the environmental degradation, and the exploitation of workers—Sarah saw it all as connected and untenable. In her heart, she envisioned a new path: a fashion line that embraced sustainability, not as an afterthought, but as its essence.

She imagined clothing that was both beautiful and built to last, made from materials that cared for the earth and its people. With a clear sense of purpose in mind, she embarked on a journey toward a more sustainable fashion landscape.

The Conceptualizer Role: Proving the Idea

Driven by her vision, Sarah immersed herself in research. She attended sustainable fashion forums, connected with environmental experts, and studied market trends. She validated her ideas against consumer data which showed a growing demand for ethical fashion. Her brand, she decided, would only use  organic, recycled materials and seek partners with manufacturers who pay fair wages. She researched costs of materials and the availability of supply chains in line with this criterion. She collected necessary supporting data and documented it all until she had proven to herself and to a close set of advisers that her product, price point and market were possible.

Organizer Role: Preparing the Blueprint

With a clear strategy, and supporting evidence, Sarah began to structure her company. She designed a business model that focused on limited, quality, timeless collections that actively sought to avoid overproduction.

She created a detailed business plan that outlined the key milestones and timelines required to establish her sustainability focused clothing brand. Sarah carefully planned the operational aspects, including supply chain management, production processes, and distribution channels.

Each process, from sourcing to shipping, was mapped out with a focus on minimizing carbon footprints and maximizing ethical practices. As she identified these processes, she shared with her small team instructions to both implement and enhance them.

Through her meticulous organization, she ensured that her brand will operate efficiently today, with room to grow tomorrow.

Investor Role: Securing the Future

Knowing that her ambitious plan needs solid financial backing, Sarah embraced the Investor Role. She turned her attention to exploring funding options.

She looks at various funding options, such as seeking investors, securing loans, or utilizing crowdfunding platforms. Ultimately, she chose and presented her business plan and financial projections to select potential investors. She had a compelling case:

a fashion brand that would achieve profitability with ethical integrity.

Her detailed, well-researched and well-organized financial forecasts and evidence of a niche market convinced several investors to back her, securing the initial capital she needed to launch her first collection.

Implementor Role: From Vision to Reality

With funding secured, Sarah transitioned into execution. She finalized her fabric choices, signed contracts with carefully selected ethical suppliers, and supervised the production process to ensure everything adhered to her high standards. Each decision, from the factory floor to the retail website, was scrutinized.

With a focus on practicality and execution, she oversaw the design process, collaborated with manufacturers, and managed the day-to-day operations of her brand. Sarah's attention to detail and commitment to quality resulted in the creation of stylish and sustainable garments that met the expectations of her target audience and the investors that supporting the endeavor.

The Implementer Role enabled her to turn her ideas into tangible products and deliver on her brand promise.

The Luminary Role: Explosive Enthusiasm

Sarah took on the Luminary Role as she enthusiastically communicated her brand's values and engaged with her growing target audience. Leveraging her communication skills and her deep understanding of her brand's mission, she relied on social media platforms, content creation, and storytelling techniques to raise awareness and grow her loyal following.

The Team Builder Role: Cultivating The Team

As her business began to flourish, Sarah saw the need for her growing team to be equally focussed on quality and minimalism. She carefully selected each new hire, not only for their skills but for their dedication to sustainability. She nurtured a company culture that valued innovation, transparency, and respect for both people and the resources.

As Sarah's sustainable clothing brand grew, she recognized the importance of building a strong and dedicated team. In her role as the Team Builder, she focused on nurturing relationships, recruiting individuals who share her passion for sustainability, and fostering a positive work culture. Sarah empowered her team members, delegated responsibilities effectively, and built a collaborative environment where creativity and innovation thrive. By assembling a talented and motivated team, she ensured the long-term success and sustainability of her brand.

Sarah's journey demonstrates how embracing and leveraging the various roles can lead to the realization of a visionary sized idea. It is also clear from this example that the ongoing success of her business depends on constantly assessing her role play to match her business needs. As the market shifts, she will perhaps need the data insights provided by the Conceptualizer Role, or more networking from her Luminary Role. She might even need to adjust her vision to incorporate a new direction using her Prophet Role.

But, and yes, I hear your objections, what if you don't have a big goal? What if you don't know what you want or where you are going? How do you know which role to play and for how long and what if you need to play roles at the same time and a hundred other questions! Learn the Seven Roles and then we will talk about how you can use them, even if and maybe especially if, you don't currently have a visionary-sized idea or big goal or even a direction.

Let's first figure out which roles are your favorites, best played, and strongest. And which aren't.

WHAT IS MY ROLESET?

The Seven Roles offer seven different mindsets with accompanying behaviors to navigate life's diverse settings. Knowing your "roleset," your strongest roles and your weaker ones, will give you an idea of how you currently or frequently approach your day, tasks, people, and more. The goal is to rank the Seven Roles in order from strongest or most used, to weakest, or least used. It is helpful to keep a single environment or situation in mind because you will likely play different roles at work than at home, for example.

Identify one or two roles that are the furthest from your comfort zone or that you are least interested in performing. These are likely your weaker roles. These roles will be more of a challenge to acquire or assume if needed. You might even wonder why you would try. But don't decide that yet. Please read on before you marginalize a role or two. The hope is to convince you of the value of practicing or at least learning to recognize all Seven Roles.

Consider how you actually think and behave while working in a specific environment rather than how you think others might perceive you or how you might wish you were. Use your actual behaviors toward goals, tasks, and relationships.

Let's look at three different approaches to help you learn your roleset.

Option 1: Quick Quiz method

Take the quiz included here. Think about a specific scenario as you answer the questions. For example, you might focus more on using the Organizer at work and the Implementor at home.

Prophet

- Do you think creatively and see things from a unique, new or different perspective?
- Are you comfortable in chaotic situations and do you adapt to change quickly?
- Are you willing to take risks and withstand criticism in pursuit of your vision?
- Do you seek ideas that challenge the status quo?

Organizer

- Are you able to break down complex tasks into manageable steps?
- Do you focus on planning out your goals?
- Are you efficient in your work?
- Are you good at multitasking? Overseeing complicated projects?

Luminary

- Are you engaging and inspiring to those around you?
- Do you have an optimistic and enthusiastic outlook on life?
- Are you communicative and able to energize those around you?
- Do you know a lot of people and have access to most of them?

Investor

- Are you strategic in your decision-making?
- Do you evaluate potential outcomes and risks before taking action?
- Are you inclusive and seek out diverse perspectives?
- Do you maintain a network of useful connections?

Team Builder

- Are you empathetic in your interactions?
- Do you value collaboration?
- Are you supportive of and trusted by others?
- Are you able to calm someone down?

Implementor

- Are you practical and task-focused?
- Do you take immediate action when you see something that needs to be done?
- Are you quick to volunteer your help?
- Do you get stuff done?

Conceptualizer

- Are you data-focused in your decision-making?
- Do you seek out new knowledge and understanding of complex issues?
- Are you curious about the world around you?
- Do you share what you learn with others?

Remember that these descriptions are simply a starting point to help with self discovery. Also, no one is limited to only one role. You will likely find that you identify with multiple roles. The important activity here is to rank them in order of how strongly or how often you play them, ideally for different environments, e.g. at home, with friends, or at work.

Option 2: Time Trial Method

A great way to learn both the roles in general and your own personal role strengths is to practice them over time. It would look like this:

UNIT II: THE SEVEN ROLES FRAMEWORK

1. Choose a role and a length of time. This could be a day, or a week or even a month if you are intent on mastering a particular role.
2. Read the chapter on that role and practice every exercise that is suggested.
3. The exercises you DON'T want to do are probably the most helpful in acquiring the role ability.

This is my favorite method. If I want to focus on expanding a role, the only way to actually measurably improve it is to repeatedly and intentionally choose it over a period of time. This is by far the most challenging method because it takes time but it is likely the most productive.

Option 3: Scale Method

The third option to assess your role strengths and weaknesses is to the take the official scale. If you would prefer this test format, go to SevenRoles.com to take the scale for a fee. Other options for learning and using the roles for different purposes are also offered there.

Get Your Money's Worth

Creating a book that speaks to every role is a challenge. After all, your preferred role for learning might not align with the role I naturally adopt when writing. However, I have strived to bridge this gap by ensuring that the contents cater in some way to every single role. To this end, the structure of this book has been planned with the Seven Roles perspectives in mind. Here's how each role's preferences have been taken into account:

For the Prophet, there are bullet style intros, checklists and chapter summaries offering a quick way to gain relevant info.

For the Organizer, the step-by-step approach laid out in the book provides both structure and a plan.

The Investor will value the insights into others and the methods to further expand their network with enriched communication skills.

The Implementer will use the practical tips and actionable steps.

For the Conceptualizer, the research-based approach to the Seven Roles will appeal to their analytical nature and desire for understanding the underlying theories and principles. Supplemental data supporting the scale development is also referenced in the appendix.

The Luminary will engage with the connection opportunities and the excitement of trying out and sharing with others something new and fun.

The Team Builder will connect with the emphasis on personal growth and a focus on others.

Which of these matter to you? This is a big clue at knowing your own role preferences. There are seven ways to look at virtually any situation or goal. You will find that each role reflects a very different perspective. Learning to see from all seven vantages will greatly expand your options and your ability to respond in the most useful way.

UNIT II: THE SEVEN ROLES FRAMEWORK

Remember, this book is more than just learning something new—it's about choosing your own personal growth and triggering change. Maybe it's strengthening a role you already rely on—or gently exploring one you've held at arm's length.

The more you understand the Seven Roles, the more boldly you'll step into who you are—and the more equipped you'll be to lead, support, and inspire those around you.

> *"It's not who you are that holds you back,*
> *it's who you think you're not."*
> —Denis Waitley

SUMMARY

This chapter introduced the Seven Roles framework, showing how it evolved from an individualized therapeutic tool to a powerful approach for teams and leaders in corporate settings. Each role—Prophet, Organizer, Luminary, Investor, Team Builder, Implementer, and Conceptualizer—was briefly described using the memorable acronym "POLITIC," a reminder of how optimal collaboration can achieve biggest goals.

Through the story of Sarah, an aspiring entrepreneur, you saw how each role plays a part in her journey. She needs and uses all seven.

You also learned three ways to discover your own roleset: the Quick Quiz Method, the Time Trial Method, and the Seven Roles Scale. Use these to identify your strongest roles—and your weakest.

For a bit of inspiration, explore the quotes sprinkled throughout the book. Each quote reflects a role's mindset—find one that resonates with you and keep it visible as a reminder of how that role 'thinks.' For example, if you're focusing on the Organizer Role, finding a favorite quote about bringing order to chaos might help keep you on track.

Ready to role? Read on!

"Everyone thinks of changing the world, but no one thinks of changing himself." -Leo Tolstoy

ONE QUICK TIP

The goal of this chapter is to motivate you to identify your roleset—to find your strongest roles and your weaker roles and rank them. Here are three simple options for you to use as you approach that goal:

1. As you learn the roles, find your favorite role and lean into it even more. Make it even better. You are already good at it, embrace it.
2. Choose your least favorite role and find someone who plays it well. Watch what they do. You will learn a surprising amount of how to play a role by simply watching others who play the role well.
3. Identify a role that is neither your strongest nor your weakest. This is often a role that you play moderately well but haven't fully developed. Pay attention to situations where this role could be beneficial and consciously practice using it. This can often lead to a more balanced and versatile roleset.

DISCUSSION THOUGHTS

1. Which of the Seven Roles do you naturally gravitate towards, and why?
2. Can you name all Seven Roles? POLITIC?
3. Describe how you take action and accomplish tasks. Do you get it done (Implementer style) or plan first (Organizer style)?

4. How do you foster team cohesion and collaboration, similar to the Team Builder role?
5. On a scale of 1 to 10, how much do you enjoy talking about money and financial matters like the Investor Role?
6. Who inspires you? What role(s) do you think they play?
7. Whether you play them or not, which roles do you value the most and why?
8. Any thoughts on which role you want to focus on first?
9. What if the people around you played different roles than they do now? Would that help you?
10. Look ahead. What is the one role you wish you played more or better? Why?

"Who looks outside, dreams. Who looks inside, awakes." -Carl Jung

---

UNIT III: THE SEVEN ROLES
YOUR ROLE YOUR CHOICE

Chapter Overview

In this section, we go on an in-depth exploration of the Seven Roles. The format for presenting each role is identical, making it easy to cross reference or jump around.

Here's the best part: this journey has no prescribed path or order. Unlike most books that follow a linear progression, the next chapters offer you the freedom to design your own learning adventure. Why? Because your curiosity and interest are your best guides here.

The roles can be explored, learned, and practiced in the order that most intrigues you.

Each role is presented in the same overall format. The chapters all begin with a story about an individual who exemplifies that specific role. These stories are an attempt to breathe life into each role and offer a relatable story to the more academic role definitions. They are

UNIT III: THE SEVEN ROLES

all based on real people and real stories so they offer specific examples of the versatility and usefulness of the roles.

Following the stories, the roles are presented in a bullet-point format for those who prefer quick, concise information. This is followed by a longer, more detailed description that explores the nuances of each role, including its motivations, strengths, and challenges.

Finally, each chapter concludes with practical exercises designed to help you play each role. These exercises include examples to help show how the role is used.

If you are ready to move your role play up a notch, an Advanced Tips section is next. Don't let it overwhelm you when you first begin learning the roles, but don't avoid it either. It's full of helpful advanced tips for maximizing your role play.

As we move from one role to another, remember to keep an open mind and heart. You may find yourself resonating with certain roles more than others, but the goal is not to categorize or limit ourselves. Think of them as tools in your toolbox, with all Seven Roles ready and available whenever you need them.

You're in charge of the journey ahead, so feel free to explore in the order that interests you most. The power lies not in the role itself, but in the ability to choose it.

You choose the changes you want, the roles you need, and the roles you play.

"We need 4 hugs a day for survival. We need 8 hugs a day for maintenance. We need 12 hugs a day for growth." -Virginia Satir

---

ENVISIONING THE PROPHET ROLE
LIVING AS A VISIONARY

Do you think creatively and see things from a unique, new or different perspective?
Are you comfortable in chaotic situations and do you adapt to change quickly?
Are you willing to take risks and withstand criticism in pursuit of your vision?
Do your ideas challenge the status quo?
This is the PROPHET ROLE!

WELCOME to the chapter on the Prophet Role—the role that looks ahead, imagines what's next, and charts the path forward. The Prophet Role isn't just about predicting the future; it's about critically assessing the present and envisioning what *could be*. It's the role that challenges what isn't working and drives meaningful change.

Mastering the Prophet Role requires perseverance and boldness. Unlike the other six roles, the Prophet needs to stand apart from group consensus to fully engage. By definition, unique ideas disrupt the status quo, and this is the role that steps up to that challenge.

This chapter is divided into three key sections:

- A look at a life with and without the Prophet Role.
- A bullet-point breakdown of key Prophet Role behaviors, followed by a detailed explanation of its traits *and* its unique communication style.
- Practical applications, advanced insights, and strategies to strengthen your ability to play this role.

Let's begin by looking at a life without the Prophet Role. Myra is a single mom, balancing remote work while raising three children. She does not actively play the Prophet Role—yet. Later in this chapter, we'll explore how Myra's life changes as she engages it.

Story Part 1: Myra

[Myra: A single mom of three school age boys.] I woke up this morning to the sound of my three boys bickering. It wasn't even 6 a.m. yet, and they were already arguing over something trivial. I dragged myself out of bed, exhausted and nowhere near ready to start the day.

We were running late—again. The boys couldn't find their homework, their shoes, or the clothes they had to wear. They're picky eaters, so packing their lunches was another challenge. I scrambled to throw together something they wouldn't leave uneaten, feeling the frustration build before the day had even begun.

The morning only got worse. The boys fought over every little thing, and I felt like a full-time referee. Keeping the peace took more energy than I had. By the time I got them to school—late—I was already running on empty.

At work, things weren't any better. I spent the day putting out fires, answering last-minute emails, and dealing with unexpected problems. Then, a massive project landed on my plate with an urgent deadline. Someone else had dropped the ball, and now it was my responsibility. I barely had time to get through my normal workload—how was I supposed to take this on too?

I don't have time or energy to think beyond the next crisis. My days are a blur of school drop-offs, endless chores, and late nights trying to catch up on work. I handle the immediate emergencies, like the sink clogging or an overdue bill, but bigger problems—things that actually matter—just keep piling up.

By the end of the day, I feel like I've accomplished nothing. Worse, I feel like I'm losing ground. I'm constantly reacting instead of making progress, and I don't even know what I'm supposed to be working toward anymore.

I want to collapse on the couch, but there's no time to rest. I still have work to do, and now I have an extra project due Friday. I don't remember the last time I got a full night's sleep. The boys start fighting over the game console, and I don't have the energy to deal with it. I close the door to muffle the noise and try to focus, keeping one ear open just in case.

It's days like these that make me feel like I'm failing as a mom. I can't see beyond the day-to-day chaos. I'm too busy managing the present to even think about the future, and my family is paying the price. And when I do stop to think—like right now—it only makes the feeling worse.

Myra's struggle isn't just about exhaustion—it's about direction. Without a clear vision for the future, every day feels like survival mode, reacting instead of leading. She's stuck in the present, unable to step back and see where she's headed.

This is where the Prophet Role makes all the difference.

HOW CAN THE PROPHET ROLE HELP YOU?

The Prophet Role helps you become the architect of your future. When you play this role, you don't just react to life—you shape what comes next. You see possibilities before others do, define a vision, and move toward it with purpose.

In relationships: When you embrace the Prophet Role in your relationships, you don't just accept things as they are but are always aiming for more. You introduce the big dreams, the path forward toward something better. It could be envisioning exciting experiences to share, or identifying areas of conflict that need to be addressed.

You're the relationship visionary—seeing the potential for what could be, first in yourself and then in others. The Prophet Role isn't just about inspiration; it's about tactical communication, knowing when to encourage and when to challenge—and also about being brave enough to initiate tough conversations when they're needed.

In your career: Professionally, the Prophet Role is about being proactive and forward-thinking. You don't wait for change—you anticipate it. You sense patterns, spot emerging trends, and recognize where things are headed before they fully materialize.

Prophets bring fresh ideas to the table, challenge outdated approaches, and push teams to think beyond the present. You might be the one suggesting an innovative project, identifying a new market opportunity, or questioning long-standing inefficiencies. This role isn't about disruption for the sake of it—it's about seeing the problems with the status quo and steering towards smarter, better solutions.

In your personal life: In your personal life, embodying the Prophet Role means you're actively creating the life you want to live. You don't drift along, waiting for things to happen—you define your goals, adjust your course as needed, and move toward a future that aligns with your vision.

Even in times of chaos or uncertainty, you're able to see the bigger picture and keep moving towards your vision. It's about finding your own path in life, no matter how unconventional or challenging, and retaining the determination and resilience to follow through with it.

The Prophet Role is embraces change, rises to the challenges produced in times of uncertainty, and is a catalyst for positive transformation.

It's a mindset of visionary thinking, tactical decision-making, and the courage to challenge what's not working.

Playing this role isn't always easy—it often means standing apart, taking risks, and navigating resistance. But when you do, you don't just improve your own life—you inspire others to see what's possible and step into their own future with purpose.

So, take a deep breath, lean into your Prophet Role, and start shaping what comes next.

"You cannot change your destination overnight, but you can change your direction overnight." — *Jim Rohn*

IF YOU PLAY THE PROPHET ROLE

If you play the Prophet Role, your vision for the future is clear. You may not know every step you need to take to get there, in fact, it is likely that you don't. But you do know where you want to end up.

This role actively assesses the way things are today while envisioning what is possible. Here are a few of the many benefits of adopting this role. Which one would help you right now?

Future Master: You can see beyond the present. By stepping back and viewing the bigger picture, you can anticipate and solve problems before they become a crisis.

Change Catalyst: You can be a change agent. By identifying shortcomings in the current system, you develop innovative modifications that can improve the ways things are.

Destination Designer: You plan for the future. By thinking ahead and visualizing the future, you can create a destination worth aiming for.

Innovation Driver: You can avoid getting stuck in the status quo. By constantly looking for new and better ways to do things, you avoid complacency and stagnation. You have a forward-thinking mindset that learns from your and others mistakes.

Relationship Enhancer: You can improve relationships. By being proactive, rather than reactive, you willingly face problems rather than ignore or avoid them. No conflict avoidance with this role.

Confidence Builder: You can build confidence in the future. By having a clear vision, you reduce anxiety about the unknown.

Life Purposed: You can create a sense of purpose. By having a long-term goal and a roadmap to get you there, you contribute to a sense of purpose by knowing what direction you are heading to.

Visionary: You are a visionary. By presenting a compelling vision for the future, you inspire and unite others.

Story Part 2: Myra

Let's look back at Myra and her life. What would it look like if she were to apply the Prophet Role to her life? Listen as she describes how she used the Prophet Role to change her life trajectory.

[Myra: Six months later.] The first step I took was to step back and really examine my life. I needed to understand why our home felt chaotic, why my boys were constantly bickering, and why I was always overwhelmed. I realized I was living in full reaction mode—constantly putting out fires but never making real progress. Survival had become my only strategy.

Once I recognized the patterns, I saw the missing piece: I wasn't shaping our future, I was just trying to survive the present. If I didn't define what I wanted our home life to be, how could I ever move toward it? I started asking myself: What does a peaceful, connected family look like? How does it feel?

With this vision in mind, I stopped just hoping things would get better and started thinking about how to make it happen. I took small but intentional steps, beginning with practical systems that could reduce the daily stress. I introduced simple morning and evening checklists so we weren't scrambling every day. I found a meal-planning system designed for kids, encouraging them to try new foods while involving them in the preparation. I took lots of small steps in the direction of my goal to have a calm and peaceful home and little by little, they helped.

I also started communicating differently with my boys. Instead of just reacting to their fights, I began explaining how their words and actions shaped our family dynamic. I helped them see that respect and teamwork weren't just rules I enforced, but values that made life better for all of us. They started taking more responsibility, and to my surprise, they actually seemed to appreciate it.

As I continued playing the Prophet Role, I saw our family dynamics shifting. The bickering decreased, and my boys began handling conflicts with more patience. Our home wasn't perfect, but it was becoming a place of connection rather than constant tension. Most importantly, I stopped feeling like I was losing ground every day.

While there are still difficult days, I now have a clearer vision for the future and the direction we are all going. I am still making decisions that support the goal of a calm and peaceful home. Playing the Prophet Role has given me the ability to imagine a better life for myself and my family.

Myra has changed the trajectory of her life—and likely, her children's lives too. As her boys grow and her circumstances evolve, she'll need to return to the Prophet Role again and again. Permanent status quo is never the goal, as those who play the Prophet Role would certainly agree. But for now, she has a clear view of the future she's navigating toward.

And while her home still has its messy moments, she walks through them with intention rather than overwhelm. That's the power of the Prophet Role: it gives us permission to pause, to imagine a better future, and to take the steps—however small—that move us toward it.

The Prophet Role isn't simply learning to dream big. It's intentionally aligning your actions with your dreams. It's recognizing the gap between where you are and where you could be—and having the courage to close it.

This next section offers bulleted descriptors for playing this role. As you read through, ask yourself:

- Which of these do I already embody?
- Which ones challenge me?
- Which could help me move forward?

Now it's time to take a closer look *Prophet Role style.*

Clear. Bold. Straight to the point.

"Stand before the people you fear and speak your mind—even if your voice shakes." —Maggie Kuhn

THE PROPHET ROLE BULLETED

Intuition is not a guess; it's an echo from the future.

Visionary of Change: The Prophet Role is a visionary of change, thriving in and managing chaos with out-of-the-box thinking.

Value-Driven: Guided by deeply held values and drawn to problems they find meaningful—this role fuels original, purposeful solutions.

Great Boundaries: Operates with others with well-defined boundaries. Yes is yes, no is no.

Imaginative: Sees beyond what currently exists, imagines what could be. This role is not constrained by what is.

Disruptor: Doesn't fear being different. Stays grounded in purpose, not popularity. Guided by vision, not group consensus.

Rapid Critique: Critiques, evaluates and often improves ideas and performance.

Outcome Predictor: Predicts the end result of the current path. Thinks about multiple, alternative paths and their potential outcomes and considers consequences before choosing.

Third Way: If something can be done this way or that way, this role finds the third, and often, the better way.

Conviction and Confidence: An unwavering conviction and confidence when presenting ideas or a vision.

Decisive: Makes decisions quickly, often relying on intuition.

Courageous & Resilient: Faces resistance with resolve. Holds steady to the vision, purpose or dream.

Direct: Prefers a direct, more blunt communication style. This role says what they mean and means what they say.

Calm Under Pressure: The Prophet Role remains steady and composed, even in stressful or challenging situations. This role isn't visibly affected by emotional excess, drama, or hyperbole, their own or anyone else's.

If this role is unused or underdeveloped:

- Lives in the moment. Tends to go with the flow.
- Does not notice or avoids problems and conflict.
- Maintains whatever the current system is because it seems safer to do that than to try to change it.
- Has no vision for the future, and often feels adrift.

If this role is overused:

- Overly critical.
- Does not encourage input.
- Offers too many changes.

THE PROPHET ROLE DESCRIBED

The Prophet Role is the master of change—driven by a vision. They are unshaken by obstacles, and relentless in the pursuit of what could be/. Prophets don't just see the future; they shape it. They analyze the present, challenge the status quo, and create solutions that redefine what's possible.

Where others see limitations, the Prophet Role sees potential. While brainstorming and idea generation exist in all Seven Roles, Prophets distinguish themselves by turning possibilities into a bold, long-term vision. They aren't constrained by what already exists or what data can currently verify. Many of their insights rely on intuition—an ability to sense opportunities and trends before they become obvious to others. Achieving large-scale change often requires a leap of faith, and Prophets are willing to take it.

Because their visions extend beyond conventional wisdom, Prophets don't rely heavily on group consensus before moving forward. They are quick to analyze and critique ideas, filtering what could work from what won't. They challenge outdated methods, ask hard questions, and refuse to settle for "this is how it's always been done." Their role isn't to maintain comfort—it's to push boundaries and inspire progress.

This decisiveness can sometimes come across as abrupt or controversial, but it emerges from a careful blend of intuition, experience, and available facts. Prophets have learned to trust their practiced 'gut feeling,' recognizing that bold moves often require stepping beyond what data alone can verify.

While others debate, Prophets commit. They trust their ability to see past temporary resistance and recognize that change often meets skepticism before it gains momentum.

The Prophet Role demands courage, resilience, and adaptability—because pursuing bold visions always comes with risks, opposition and setbacks. But Prophets are undeterred. They adjust their approach when needed, drawing on inner conviction to keep moving forward. They don't wait for permission to act; they forge ahead and let their results speak for themselves.

Ultimately, Prophets ignite change by believing in something before it exists. Their unwavering sense of purpose is contagious, drawing others toward a shared vision of something greater.

In a world that often clings to the comfort of sameness, the Prophet Role is the force that dares to ask, "What if there's a better way?"

"When something is important enough, you do it even if the odds are not in your favor." -Elon Musk

---

THE PROPHET ROLE PRACTICED

This section offers practical activities with examples to help you practice the Prophet Role. There are three steps to master this role, beginning with the most critical first step: adopting the Prophet mindset.

A mindset is the mental framework that guides your thoughts, decisions, and behaviors. It's like your mind's operating system, shaping how you perceive and react to the world around you. Changing your mindset means reprogramming this operating system to align with your goals.

Step 1: Adopt the Mindset of the Prophet Role

As you step into the Prophet Role, it is important to adopt the following thought processes, especially if they are unfamiliar or underplayed by you:

Confidence and Decisiveness: Stand firm in your beliefs, make decisions, and own the outcome.

Courageous and Resilient: Do not fear criticism or backlash; instead, use them as fuel to sharpen or correct your vision.

Unwavering Conviction: Trust in the power of your ideas and the change they can bring about.

Value-Driven: Know what you believe. Know why it matters. Anchor your decisions and ideas to your personal values.

Direct Communication: Speak your mind, be clear and precise with your words, and mean what you say.

Keeping these in mind as you move on to step 2 as this will greatly enhance your ability to play the Prophet Role. If you practice *thinking* like the role, you will more easily learn to *act* like the role.

Step 2: Choose an Activity to Practice the Role

This next section contains a range of activities designed to help you embody and practice the Prophet Role. When you choose an activity, focus first on the mindset traits above. Each activity aligns with the characteristics of the Prophet and will help you refine and internalize these traits. It often helps to choose the activity you are least wanting to do.

Step 3: Repeat

The more you practice, the more adept you will become at embodying the Prophet Role.

Remember, transformation doesn't happen overnight; be patient with yourself and stay committed to the process.

"The future belongs to those who believe in the beauty of their dreams." -Eleanor Roosevelt

PRACTICAL EXERCISES: PROPHET

Here are some specific strategies for developing and mastering the Prophet Role. If you rarely play this role, start by choosing one of the exercises and then practice it for a week. If you pair it with a mindset trait from the previous section, you will increase your learning.

For example, combine the first exercise "Practice out-of-the-box thinking" with a mindset of confidence and decisiveness. This would mean that as you think of ideas, you would focus on sharing them with confidence and decisiveness. When you feel comfortable with that, move on to the next trait, that of being courageous and resilient.

This is clearly more challenging as it means that you will choose to share an idea that is likely to be rejected. How do you handle overcoming the fear of sharing your ideas? How do you handle your disappointment if an idea is rejected? Thinking like the Prophet Role does not mean you are fearless, it does mean that fear does not stop you.

As you pair how this role thinks to practice activities, you can learn to identify and navigate your own mind blocks.

Practice Out-of-the-Box Thinking: Challenge yourself to think outside the box and come up with creative solutions to problems and work to see things from different perspectives. Look for opportunities to try something in a different way than you always have.

Patch demonstrates creative problem-solving and a willingness to challenge conventional thinking. Recently, his team faced a major hurdle: their AI models were slowing down under heavy data loads, making real-time decision-making difficult.

While typical solutions include scaling up cloud resources, Patch proposed a different approach—experimenting with edge AI models, which process data closer to where it's generated instead of relying entirely on the cloud. Though unconventional, this method reduced delays, improved efficiency, and significantly lowered costs, allowing the AI models to handle complex data far more smoothly.

This ability to see beyond the obvious and explore creative solutions exemplifies the Prophet Role, proving that true innovation often comes from questioning the usual way of doing things and thinking out-of-the-box.

Communicate Directly: Less is more. Practice what you will say before you say it. As you practice, constantly think of making it shorter, clearer, more direct.

Edward has learned that his manager often plays the Prophet Role. Wanting to ensure that his input is well received, he sends his updates in a summarized bullet form style followed by the details. This accommodates for his manager's Prophet Role style who values the "get to the point" approach while allowing Edward a means to share necessary information.

This role is the master of economical speech. Learn to speak your mind with clarity and precision of words.

Be brief, be bright, be gone. —President Woodrow Wilson

Critique your Goals and Visions: Make a habit of analyzing your goals and visions, and think critically about how they will turn out.

Look for potential pitfalls and consider different scenarios, including worst-case scenarios. Take a few extra minutes to practice evaluating ideas from all angles and considering how they will work in different situations.

Suzanne's boss had just offered her the kind of promotion people dream about—more responsibility, more visibility, and a significant salary increase. It was the kind of opportunity that would normally prompt an automatic "yes." But instead of jumping in, Suzanne paused and turned to her Prophet Role for critiquing.

She started by examining her deeper motivations. Was she pursuing this role because it aligned with her long-term purpose—or because it looked impressive on paper?

Next, Suzanne imagined how the role might feel six months in. She knew the job would mean more travel, longer hours, and leading a team through a period of uncertainty. Could she still be the kind of leader—and person—she wanted to be under that pressure?

She thought about worst-case scenarios too. What if accepting the promotion distanced her from the work she actually loved doing? What if it drained her time and energy without delivering the meaning she hoped for?

Rather than rushing, Suzanne used her Prophet Role to ask herself the kind of questions that don't show up in a pros and cons list:

Does this next step move me closer to the life I want—or just farther from what I've built?

Ultimately, Suzanne took the job. But she negotiated for a few key changes—delegation support, greater autonomy, and a defined review period—so that the new role could work *with* her values, not against them.

Embrace Change: Prophets are often at their best when things are in flux and chaos arises. Practice welcoming change at every stage of life. Come up with new ideas that work in your unpredictable circumstances. This can include taking on new challenges, working with diverse groups of people, or pursuing new interests.

Robert has always embodied the Prophet Role well, not just embracing change but actively seeking it. As he approaches retirement, a time that many might see as a winding down, Robert views it as an exciting new chapter.

Rather than stepping away, Robert looks at retirement as a time to lean in. He explores opportunities where his experience and insights can make a difference—whether through mentoring, volunteering, or pursuing personal interests that energize him.

With his forward-thinking approach, Robert welcomes this phase of life with enthusiasm, constantly asking, "What's next?" His openness to change allows him to embrace the future with optimism, finding fulfillment in the new opportunities ahead.

Disrupt the Status Quo: Look for opportunities to challenge the status quo and improve upon existing processes. This can involve taking risks, questioning assumptions, and trying new things.

Lucia is a busy mother of three kids who was constantly frustrated by the amount of garbage her family produced. Every week, she would drag multiple bags of garbage to the curb, and it seemed like there was always more to throw away. She started to think about the amount of waste they were producing and wondered if there was a way to reduce it.

She began by looking at their trash to get an idea of what it all was. She discovered that nearly half of their waste could be composted. She soon discovered that it was easier than she thought to start a compost bin in her backyard. She involved their kids in the process, teaching them about the importance of reducing waste.

At first, the neighbors were skeptical and thought it was a strange idea. But as they saw the results, they became more curious and started asking questions. Lucia and her family showed them how to compost, and soon other families in the neighborhood started their own compost bins.

It wasn't long before the entire neighborhood started to notice a difference. The amount of garbage that was being picked up each week started to decrease. And small gardens began to pop up, feeding on the new compost. Lucia and her family had changed the normal way of doing things for a better way.

Amplify Big Picture Thinking: Think about how different pieces fit together to form a coherent whole, and consider the long-term impact of the status quo and of how your ideas will impact it. Practice taking a step back and looking at the larger context of situations and considering how different pieces fit together. Focus on the end goal and work backwards to develop a plan to achieve it.

Elon envisions a future where technology pushes boundaries—not just in one area, but across multiple industries. He sees beyond individual innovations, recognizing that truly transformative change requires an entire ecosystem—from advanced AI and infrastructure to regulatory frameworks and global accessibility.

Rather than getting discouraged by how ambitious or unattainable his goals might seem, he works methodically to develop each piece needed to bring them to life.

By focusing on the bigger picture, Elon connects each step—from pioneering electric vehicles and self-driving technology to building a planetary internet network and planning for Mars colonization—so that every effort moves toward his long-term vision. No matter how outlandish his ideas might seem, he remains committed, constantly working to turn the impossible into reality.

Value-Driven: As you make purpose driven life decisions, anchor them with your personal values and the problems you consider significant.

Pam answers a deep calling to give back to her community, but for her, volunteering isn't just about filling time—it's about making a meaningful impact. She approaches each opportunity with intention, ensuring that her efforts align with her core values.

When several organizations reach out for her support, she takes a moment to reflect. A high-profile charity is hosting a large fundraiser, and another well-known nonprofit is looking for volunteers to help. Both are worthy causes, but Pam knows where her heart leads her. She is drawn to places where she can build real relationships and see the direct impact of her work.

She chooses to dedicate her time to a small community outreach program supporting missionary families in need. Through this role, she provides practical assistance, encouragement, and a sense of home to those serving far from theirs.

For Pam, playing the Prophet Role means making choices that reflect her values and fulfill her deeper purpose.

Build Courage: Pursuing a Prophet Role vision often involves taking risks and pushing boundaries. Practice taking risks and standing up for your ideas, even in the face of negativity or opposition.

Andy had always been passionate about writing and believed in his unique style. But after submitting his manuscript to publishers, he faced rejection after rejection, with feedback that his ideas were too unconventional.

Rather than give up, Andy embraced the Prophet Role. He stood firm in his vision and decided to take a risk by self-publishing. Without the backing of a traditional publisher, Andy used online platforms to share his story, slowly building a loyal readership.

His persistence paid off. Word of his work spread, gaining momentum and catching the attention of a major publisher. By standing up for his ideas and pushing boundaries, Andy proved that success often comes from taking risks and believing in your vision, even when others doubt you.

Develop Strong Conviction: Take the time to thoroughly evaluate your ideas and visions, and don't present them until you yourself are fully convinced. Practice speaking with conviction and confidence especially when offering your thoughts.

Sophie was a high school student, shy and reserved. One day as she was walking to school, she noticed a group of people loitering on the corner, selling drugs and causing a sense of unease to all who passed by. She was even more concerned when she realized that this was also the path the elementary school kids took. She gathered the courage to speak up about the issue and proposed a plan to make the area safer.

Despite her natural timidity, she felt so strongly about the situation that she confidently shared her idea with the school board, local authorities and the community. With her unwavering conviction, Sophie's plan was implemented and the neighborhood was improved for students.

Dream Big: Envision a future that may seem unattainable or even improbable. Take bold steps to transform this vision into reality, embracing the journey with determination and creativity.

Aaren dreams of becoming a life coach—something that feels both exhilarating and daunting. She envisions a future where she empowers individuals to navigate their own challenges and discover their true potential. But making this dream a reality means stepping away from the security of her current job and into the unknown.

At first, doubt lingers. Can she really make this work? Will people trust her enough to seek her guidance? But embracing her Prophet Role, Aaren refuses to let fear dictate her future. She begins laying the groundwork.

She carves out time in her already packed schedule to take courses, attends networking events, and begins offering discounted coaching sessions to friends and colleagues. These early experiences fuel her confidence and confirm what she already knows deep down—helping others unlock their potential is exactly what she wants to do.

Increase Resilience: A significant goal or vision is often a challenging and unpredictable process. The Prophet Role must be resilient and adaptable in the face of setbacks and obstacles. They learn from failure and are able to pick themselves up and keep going. Notice how you handle setbacks. What can you do to handle them more productively?

Benjamin has wanted to start a nonprofit to help underprivileged children gain access to quality education.

But turning a vision into reality wasn't easy. Securing funding was an uphill battle, and many of the people he reached out to were hesitant to get involved. At times, it felt like every door he knocked on remained closed. The challenges were daunting, and doubt crept in, but Benjamin refused to let setbacks define his journey.

Instead, he adapted. He refined his message and sought new opportunities. He spent long hours applying for grants, attending networking events, and sharing his vision with anyone willing to listen. Rejection became a familiar part of the process, but rather than seeing it as failure, he used it as fuel to push forward.

Little by little, his efforts started to pay off. Small donations turned into larger ones, volunteers stepped forward, and his vision gained momentum. What once seemed impossible was now taking shape—not because the path was easy, but because Benjamin had the resilience to keep going.

By practicing these behaviors and consistently using the Prophet mindset, you can strengthen your Prophet Role and imagine, create, and pursue big, audacious dreams.

"The best way to predict the future is to create it." -Peter Drucker

ADVANCED TIPS FOR PLAYING THE PROPHET ROLE

Are you ready to take this role to the next level? While the Prophet Role can be rewarding, acquiring it is not without its challenges. Here are some common obstacles that can arise when pursuing or promoting your Prophet Role, and some straightforward strategies for overcoming them.

Slow Down

If you are playing the Prophet Role, it's important to keep in mind that not everyone will understand or immediately embrace your new vision. The strength of this role is the ability to see out into the distance. This is also the weakness of this role because others might not see where you are aiming. Therefore, it's essential to communicate your ideas in a way that is clear, direct, and understandable.

Here are some tips for communicating like a Prophet:

Start with the end in mind: Before you begin communicating your new vision, take some time to fully develop and clarify the idea in your own mind. Consider the end goal and what steps will be necessary to get there. This will allow you to present a more cohesive and structured plan to others.

Use plain language: Avoid using complex terminology or jargon that may be unfamiliar or confusing to others. Instead, use plain language that is clear and straightforward, and that conveys your vision in a way that is easily understandable.

Provide context: When introducing a new vision, it's important to provide context and background information. This helps others to better understand the reasoning and rationale behind your vision, and to see how it fits into the larger context of an organization or a project.

Give People Time: Be mindful of the pace at which you communicate your ideas. While you may be excited about your vision, it's important to slow down and give others a chance to absorb and process the new direction you are proposing. Changing people's minds and inspiring them to pursue a new vision takes time especially if they play the Organizer and Implementor Roles for your ideas.

Listen: Communication is a two-way street, and it's important to actively listen to others' questions and feedback. This helps you to understand their concerns and objections, and to respond in a way that is clear and meaningful. It is up to you to make sure your vision is understood.

By using these tips and communicating your new vision in a clear, direct, and understandable way, you can help others to better understand and embrace your ideas. Make sure you thoroughly critique your own ideas before you present them, ensuring confidence in the face of questions or objections.

Slow down, give context, and listen to others to ensure that your vision is effectively communicated and understood by all.

"The most valuable of all talents is that of never using two words when one will do."
-Thomas Jefferson

Partner with Other Roles

To maximize the impact of the Prophet Role—and avoid some of its common pitfalls—it's beneficial to pair it with other roles. The Prophet Role thrives on vision and forward thinking, but at times, it can come across as blunt, abstract, or overwhelming to others. Strategic role-pairing can help bridge these gaps.

For example, Prophets often communicate in a direct, no-nonsense manner, which can sometimes feel dismissive or abrupt. Partnering with the **Team Builder Role** can soften this approach. The Team Builder emphasizes collaboration, trust, and emotional intelligence, helping ensure that the Prophet's vision is communicated in a way that invites buy-in rather than resistance.

Similarly, the Prophet Role values brevity and rapid decision-making, which can be frustrating for those who need more context. Pairing with the **Conceptualizer Role** can help here. Taking time to articulate supporting details, research, and potential outcomes can make the vision more tangible and easier for others to grasp.

Finally, sharing a bold vision without a clear path forward can leave people feeling skeptical or overwhelmed. Partnering with the **Organizer Role** helps to break down the grand idea into actionable steps, even if only in broad strokes. While a Prophet doesn't need to have every detail mapped out, offering a structured outline can make the vision feel more achievable and inspire confidence in others.

By understanding the tendencies of the Prophet Role and recognizing the role preferences of your audience, you can tailor your approach to ensure your vision is not only seen but embraced. Effective role-pairing strengthens your ability to lead change and turn ideas into reality.

Dare to see differently. The future depends on it.

ENVISIONING THE PROPHET ROLE

This Way

In a world where chaos holds reign,
Stands a Prophet, unfettered by the mundane.
Not the status quo, nor the trodden track,
But the new and unproven is their knack.

An idea, a vision, they deftly unpack,
In the realm of the unknown, they do not lack.
Compelling visions, they artistically spin,
Inviting others, to their journey within.

They walk ahead where others delay,
Lighting a torch to show the way.
Though misunderstood, they still press on,
For the birth of change begins with one.

In the world of the future, they etch a new mark,
Their bold ideas serving as the critical spark.
With courage and resilience leading the way,
Their belief in the vision, keep doubts at bay.

With clarity, they speak, their voice unbroken,
Inspiring others, by the dream they've awoken.
In the Prophet's gaze, we find strength, we find hope,
Guiding us forward, offering a safety rope.

SUMMARY

In this chapter, we explored the **Prophet Role**—the visionary, the risk-taker, the one who sees beyond the present to imagine what's possible.

Let's review this chapter Prophet Role style, which is to say, let's get to the point.

First, we looked at the defining characteristics which included:

- The ability to imagine bold and innovative ideas
- The importance of thinking outside the box
- The courage and resilience to challenge the status quo

Myra's story was shared to illustrate what life might look like when the Prophet Role is avoided and how it might change once it's engaged.

Next we looked at some of the benefits of playing the Prophet Role including its ability to:

- Inspire and motivate others
- Drive innovative change
- Push boundaries for themselves and for those around them

To develop this role, we outlined strategies to help you practice whether you are new to this role or already play it often. This included instructions on how to:

- Cultivate a Prophet mindset by embracing risk and thinking long-term
- Develop conviction by strengthening your ideas
- Pair this role strategically to avoid isolation or misunderstanding

Overall, the key takeaway for this chapter is two-fold:

1. Mastering the Prophet Role isn't just about having ideas—it's about the courage to act on them.
2. With insight, perseverance, and wise strategic role-pairing, the Prophet Role is the force for transformation that shapes the future.

And that is a chapter summary—Prophet style.

Dream big. Then make it happen.

ONE QUICK TIP

One of the key aspects of the Prophet Role is having a clear and compelling vision. This begins with you. Spend time thinking about what you want to achieve and even more importantly, why it's important to you.

Learn to brainstorm new ideas or solutions on the fly. Set aside 10-15 minutes each day to jot down ideas or problems that need solutions.

The goal is not to solve the problem or produce perfect ideas but rather to get in the habit of looking at problems as opportunities.

You can level this up by critiquing your own ideas and then sharing your thoughts with others. This allows you practice handling objections and idea rejection.

Remember, the Prophet Role critiques ideas as well as creates them. Both idea generation and realistic critique are necessary to produce dreams worth pursuing.

SPOKEN LIKE A PROPHET

Being in the Prophet Role isn't a choice, it's a necessity. The marketplace, the world, it's not just competitive, it's chaotic. But I don't see the chaos as a problem. I see it as a blank slate on which I can imagine the future. The world, you see, is never static, never even settled. And for me, that's the best part.

I tend to consider the changes on the horizon, even before they emerge. That's my forte—I'm not content with the way things are, nor am I afraid of the disruption that comes with change. I actually enjoy questioning the way things are. Why are we doing it this way? Where are we heading? What could we do better? What's next?

In my quest for a better tomorrow, I often find myself being the opposing voice in the room. I am quick to critique ideas, mine and others. Sometimes that reveals a great idea and sometimes it reveals the problems with an idea. But it isn't about poking holes in ideas. The magic truly happens when we find that elusive third way, that alternative solution which was overlooked in the this-way-or-that-way dilemma.

My decisions might seem quick, even impulsive to some, but I think long and hard about ideas before I share them. I consider the consequences, especially the unintended consequences of decisions. Frankly, I wish others did more of that—to think a bit longer about where decisions lead and what collateral damage there might be. I might not be the best brainstormer when I am in this role, but that is because I believe that if I have the same opinion as the group, I may as well not have an opinion at all.

And yes, as you might imagine, taking the road less traveled does require a fair amount of resilience. I have faced my share of adversity, criticism, and skepticism when I share a new idea. It's not always easy to stand alone, to voice ideas that might be ahead of their time or outside the "normal" way of doing things. I think of "normal" as the problem. There is always a better way, the goal is to find it.

Communication is key in my role. I mean what I say and say what I mean and value that in others. I believe in cutting through the drama and exaggeration to focus on the essence of the message. I really don't have time or patience for gossip or hearsay.

For me, the Prophet Role is not just about promoting change, it's about having the boldness to challenge the way things are, the courage to share a new way, and the conviction to see it through. I don't have favorites but if I did, this role would be the one I would choose.

"The future belongs to those who see possibilities before they become obvious." — John Sculley

---

PLANNING THE ORGANIZER ROLE
LIVING ORGANIZED

*Are you able to break down complex tasks into manageable steps?
Do you focus on planning out your goals?
Are you efficient in your work?
Are you good at multitasking? Overseeing complicated projects?
This is the ORGANIZER ROLE!*

IN THIS CHAPTER, we step into the amazingly well-ordered world of the Organizer Role. Whether you're planning a family reunion, managing multiple complicated projects, or simply trying to bring order to the chaos of daily life, the Organizer Role is your key to success. Those who master this role ensure plans are in place, details are handled, and everything runs like a well-oiled machine.

We'll start by exploring the perks of playing the Organizer Role, from boosting productivity and managing time like a pro to developing effective systems and delegating tasks with confidence.

Next, we'll break down what defines this role—the essential traits, habits, and skills that make an Organizer so effective.

For those ready to level up, the advanced tips section will help you refine your planning skills and master the art of delegation, ensuring you're not just organizing—but optimizing.

By the time we've finished, you will have a clearer understanding of what the Organizer Role is all about, and be equipped with the tools you need to take this role skill to the next level.

Let's take a look at Harvey, a talented leader whose lack of the Organizer Role threatened everything he had worked for.

Story Part 1: Harvey

[Harvey: A 50 something sales manager.] Harvey was a smart, likable, sales manager at a Fortune 100 company. His people skills and deep understanding of the company's systems had helped him climb the corporate ladder quickly, making him a tremendous asset to the company.

But Harvey had one critical flaw that cast a shadow over his strengths: he was terrible at organization.

His office was a disaster—piles of papers covered his desk, sticky notes were everywhere, and his computer desktop was a maze of unorganized files. Ironically, the man responsible for leading a high-performing sales team was drowning in his own disorganization.

The signs were everywhere:

- *Emails? Sent sporadically, often overlooked.*
- *Meetings? Scheduled at the last minute.*
- *Sales tracking? He ignored available tools, relying on sticky notes and memory instead.*
- *Team evaluations? Rarely conducted—he relied on intuition rather than measurable performance metrics.*

Harvey's lack of organization created constant inefficiencies. Bottlenecks in needed resources, missed deadlines, and frustrated team members became the norm. He struggled to delegate, holding onto tasks instead of empowering his team, which left him overloaded and his team underutilized.

Everyone liked Harvey. But as his disorganization increasingly overshadowed his value, the company began to question whether his strengths could outweigh the growing cost of his inefficiencies.

If Harvey couldn't change, his future at the company was uncertain.

Harvey's struggle wasn't just about misplaced files or last-minute meetings—it was about lost potential. Without organization, even the most talented individuals can find themselves overwhelmed, inefficient, and even, stuck.

So, how can embracing the Organizer Role make a difference? Let's explore how this role can enhance your relationships, your career, and your personal growth.

HOW CAN THE ORGANIZER ROLE HELP YOU?

The Organizer Role isn't just about neat desks and color-coded calendars—it's about efficiency, clarity, and control over the things that matter. Whether in relationships, your career, or personal development, strengthening this role can reduce stress, improve decision-making, and create space for what truly matters.

In Relationships

Organization isn't just a solo skill—it benefits those around you. Whether planning family events, managing household responsibilities, or simply ensuring quality time with loved ones, the Organizer Role helps create structure without rigidity.

- You keep track of important dates, events, and commitments, ensuring that nothing slips through the cracks.
- You create smooth routines that reduce daily chaos, making life easier for everyone involved.

- Your ability to anticipate needs helps prevent last-minute stress, allowing time for more meaningful interactions and events.

In relationships, the Organizer Role ensures that plans run smoothly and loved ones feel supported.

In Your Career

Professionally, the Organizer Role is a game-changer. It ensures that tasks don't just get done—they get done efficiently and effectively.

- You prioritize tasks strategically, ensuring the most important work gets done first.
- You set realistic deadlines and meet them, establishing yourself as reliable and capable.
- You create repeatable systems that improve workflow, making you (and your team) more productive over time.

Employers and colleagues recognize the value of an Organizer—someone who can turn chaos into clarity and help teams function smoothly.

In Personal Development

Even outside of work and relationships, playing the Organizer Role can help you achieve personal goals with greater ease.

- You set clear goals and break them down into manageable steps.
- You create realistic schedules that keep you accountable.
- You avoid procrastination by developing systems that make life progress inevitable.

The bottom line? The Organizer Role doesn't just help you get things done—it helps you get the *right* things done, at the *right* time, in the *right* way.

Read on for more benefits for those who scale up on this role.

"Order brings peace of mind, and preparation brings confidence."

IF YOU PLAY THE ORGANIZER ROLE

The Organizer Role, when understood and well-applied, can be tremendously beneficial in all areas of your life. Here are a few of the advantages you will acquire if you play this role. Which would help you most this week?

Eradicate Chaos: You can bring order to chaos. You streamline processes and systems making work easier and more efficient.

Champion Dreams: Organizers excel at setting and achieving big dreams. They understand how to break them down into clear, actionable plans. By adopting the Organizer Role, you increase your chances of implementing and achieving your Prophet sized dreams.

Harness Strengths: You are excellent at ensuring that the right people are working on the right tasks. You know who is good at what and how they can be a part of achieving the greater goal.

De-Stress Manager: Chaos and disorder can lead to increased stress and confusion. This role is the stress reducer for you and others too.

Elevate Confidence: As you become more organized and see the positive effects of your efforts, your confidence will grow too.

Unite Effort: By effectively managing projects and ensuring that everyone is working together smoothly, you build strong, cooperative relationships with colleagues, family, and friends.

Lead by Systems: The Organizer Role naturally lends itself to organizational management. The skills you learn—delegating, planning, and coordinating—are key leadership skills. As you grow in your Organizer Role, you can also grow as a leader.

Remember, while the Organizer Role has numerous benefits, the goal is not to be a perfect Organizer but to use the strengths of this role to complement your unique personality and your unique situation.

Let's see how Harvey put the Organizer Role strengths to work for him and the not at all surprising results.

Story Part 2: Harvey

[Harvey: 3 months later.] After a particularly chaotic quarter-end, Harvey found himself drained and overwhelmed. He knew something had to change. One evening, he came across an article about the Organizer Role and its impact on both professional and personal success. As he read, he recognized himself in the description—but not in a good way. He realized that his lack of structure wasn't just making his life harder; it was holding back his team and his career. It was time for a change.

Harvey started with his own workspace. He cleared out unnecessary clutter, organized his files—both physical and digital—and implemented simple systems to keep everything in order. It was a small shift, but immediately, he felt more in control.

Next, he turned his attention to his team. He introduced structured weekly meetings, set clear expectations, and started using a project management tool to track tasks and deadlines. Instead of relying on scattered notes and last-minute decisions, Harvey ensured that everyone had access to the same information, creating alignment.

As he built these new habits, Harvey realized another major flaw in his previous approach—his reluctance to delegate. He had always taken on too much himself, believing it was the fastest way to get things done. Now, he began assigning tasks based on his team members' strengths, trusting them to handle responsibilities. Not only did this lighten his workload, but it also empowered his team, increasing engagement and morale.

Harvey also started analyzing performance using data and measurable outcomes. Instead of relying on intuition alone, he used key metrics to assess progress, spot inefficiencies, and adjust strategies as needed. When obstacles arose, he was proactive in addressing them rather than reacting at the last minute.

Over time, the results spoke for themselves. Deadlines were met consistently, the team was more engaged, and the quality of work improved across the board. Harvey's transformation was evident—not only to himself but to those around him. His team admired his shift and even began adopting some of his strategies, inspired by his example.

And it wasn't just his work life that improved. With better organization and time management, Harvey had more time for himself and his family. His stress levels dropped, and for the first time in a long time, he truly enjoyed his work and his personal time.

By embracing the Organizer Role, Harvey transformed his life. His journey illustrates how the Organizer can turn chaos into order, inefficiency into productivity, and dissatisfaction into satisfaction.

The next section offers a bullet form view of the Organizer Role's traits and behaviors followed by a more detailed description. As you read through the content, think of people you know that demonstrate the behaviors. Role models offer the best examples for role behaviors.

"Planning is essential." -J. K. Rowling

THE ORGANIZER ROLE BULLETED

Plans are the blueprints for success.

The Organizer Role is defined by a set of key characteristics and behaviors, which include:

Chaos Controller: Brings order out of chaos, excelling at organizing spaces and systems, whether at home or in a professional setting.

Time Master: Utilizes time management tools to enhance personal and team productivity, preventing over-scheduling.

Plan Advocate: Plans before starting any task or project, ensuring that the right tools and resources are in place.

Progress Detective: Assesses progress and devises plans for improvement, whether for household chores, personal tasks, or team performance.

Efficiency Expert: Enjoys the process of optimizing for efficiency.

Barrier Buster: Actively removes obstacles, impediments, and inefficiencies, streamlining processes for smoother operations.

Team Tuner: Engages team members who can contribute to the workload, tracking their performance for continued development.

Process Pro: Skilled at problem solving and optimizing task synergy within a group, often focusing on the workflow and process rather than the individuals involved.

Administrative Architect: Develops and implements detailed administrative process flow inspection plans as needed.

If this role is unused or underdeveloped:

- Struggles with deadlines, processes, or project management.
- Insufficient delegation.

- Inefficiency resulting in chaos.

If this role is overused:

- Overemphasis on rules.
- Unaware of impact of processes on people.
- Micromanaging.

THE ORGANIZER ROLE DESCRIBED

Mastering the Organizer Role presents a unique journey distinct from the other roles. Unlike the Implementor, Luminary, or indeed any other role where the behaviors largely mirror each other across personal and professional domains, the Organizer Role brings a greater specificity to different arenas of life.

Therefore, we'll delve into the Organizer Role from three different perspectives. You may need to add a different area or more focus for your use to reflect specific hobbies, projects or people. Use the examples that follow to help develop your Organizer Role where you need it most.

The areas chosen here are Personal, Familial, and Professional. You may find that you are great in one area and not so great in another. The aim is to equip you with the necessary tools to expand your Organizer Role precisely where you need it most.

Personal

Playing the Organizer Role on a personal level involves effectively managing individual resources, including time, energy, and environment.

Time mastery is a crucial aspect. As an Organizer, it's not just about filling a calendar with tasks. The focus is on understanding the duration of each task, prioritizing them based on their significance and urgency, and avoiding overcommitment. Organizers recognize the importance of leaving room for rest, relaxation, and unexpected events. They utilize tools like digital calendars and task management apps to manage their time and tasks effectively. Their efficient time management often earns the admiration of others.

Personal boundaries are another key Organizer attribute. This includes identifying and voicing one's limits and assertively communicating these boundaries to others. Saying no prevents being overwhelmed. The Organizer approach helps maintain mental and physical well-being and ensures that tasks receive the attention and energy they require.

Organizers also excel in establishing efficient routines. They understand the value of consistent routines in achieving personal productivity and stability. Whether it's organizing a home office or maintaining a regular exercise schedule, an Organizer's love of structure is evident in routines.

Finally, the Organizer Role…organizes. Adhering to the mantra, "A place for everything, and everything in its place," Organizers create systems for storing items, declutter regularly, and maintain a clean, orderly living environment. This facilitates easy location of items and reduces that 'where is it' frustration.

Familial

In a home setting, the Organizer Role is essential in managing the household and balancing the schedules of multiple individuals. This role involves ensuring that all household tasks, from chores to bills to meal prep, are taken care of in a systematic, efficient manner.

The Organizer in a family setting often takes the lead in developing and managing the family's schedule. This includes coordinating daily routines, extracurricular activities, appointments, and social events. They take into account each family member's individual needs and commitments, ensuring that everyone knows where they need to be and when. They often make use of tools such as shared calendars or scheduling apps to keep everyone on the same page.

In addition to scheduling, the Organizer is adept at creating systems to manage household tasks. They might develop a chore chart that divides tasks among family members, create a meal planning system to streamline grocery shopping and cooking, or set up automatic payments for recurring bills. These systems help to distribute responsibilities and ensure that no important tasks are overlooked.

Furthermore, the Organizer Role also plays a crucial role in maintaining the living environment. They understand the impact of a clean and organized space on everyone's well-being and productivity.

Therefore, they might take charge of decluttering efforts, create effective storage solutions, or implement a regular cleaning schedule. Their aim is to create a living space where everyone can relax or thrive.

Organizers are often the ones who plan social events among friends, as they are skilled at coordinating schedules, arranging venues, and managing details like food and entertainment. They ensure everyone has a great time without any hiccups, thanks to their thorough planning and foresight.

In essence, playing the Organizer Role at home with family and friends involves creating and managing systems that help life run smoothly. It requires adaptability, foresight, and a knack for coordinating many moving parts. When executed well, this role significantly contributes to a harmonious and well-functioning living environment.

Professional

At work, the Organizer Role takes on operational significance as it involves streamlining systems and ensuring efficiency across the board. Organizers are obstacle-solvers and strategic planners, which positions them ideally to handle complex projects, orchestrate workflows, and ensure the team works cohesively towards its goals.

A key facet of the Organizer's role at work involves project management. They are adept at breaking down complex tasks into manageable chunks and creating clear, detailed plans of action. They set timelines, allocate resources, assign tasks, and monitor progress, making sure every team member knows what they need to do and when. They also ensure that the project stays on track and troubleshoot any issues that arise along the way.

Beyond advancing projects, Organizers play a crucial role in overall process management. They are constantly on the lookout for ways to make workflows more efficient. They scrutinize existing processes, identify bottlenecks or redundancies, and implement solutions to streamline operations. This might involve introducing new tools or technologies, redefining roles and responsibilities, or redesigning processes altogether.

Organizers excel at managing and allocating resources efficiently. Whether it's budget, personnel, or time, they know how to use what's available to achieve maximum productivity and results. This resourcefulness and strategic thinking often make them valued players in roles such as administrators, operations managers, and logistical coordinators.

In team settings, Organizers are often the cohesion that holds the project together. They coordinate communication, facilitate collaboration, and ensure everyone is working in sync. They ensure deadlines are met, expectations are clear, and the team remains motivated and focused on the goal.

Moreover, the Organizer's capacity to anticipate potential issues and devise contingency plans is invaluable in a professional setting. Their proactive nature and ability to plan for the unexpected keep the team prepared for any curveballs and reduce the risk of unmet deadlines or unsatisfactory results.

The Organizer Role in the workplace creates structure, enhancing efficiency, and managing complexity. It's about guiding projects to successful completion, optimizing processes, and if managerial, guides a team to function effectively. With their unique blend of strategic thinking, detailed planning, and problem-solving prowess, Organizers are instrumental in driving organizational success.

In summary, the Organizer Role is multifaceted and vital, bringing order to chaos and ensuring tasks are well-managed. In every aspect of life, whether it be professional, familial or personal, the Organizer Role brings structure and efficiency—preparing pathways to success.

Where can the Organizer Role help you? The next section offers practical activities with examples to help you practice this important role.

THE ORGANIZER ROLE PRACTICED

There are three steps to master this role, beginning with the most critical first step: adopting the Organizer mindset.

A mindset is like the navigation system that guides your thoughts, decisions, and behaviors. It's your mind's GPS, directing how you interact with the world around you. To embody the Organizer Role, you need to recalibrate your navigation system and adopt its mindset.

Step 1: Adopt the Mindset of the Organizer Role

As you seek to embody the Organizer Role, practice thinking in the following ways:

A Planner: You always plan before you start. "Winging it" is not in the Organizer vocabulary. If you can't picture and plan for the finished result, you are not playing the Organizer Role.

Chaos Controller: You welcome disorder as long as you have the authority, desire, and time to organize it.

Time Mastery: Time works for you. You schedule your time and if given the opportunity, you can help others schedule their time as well.

Efficiency Obsession: Better, faster, smoother, easier: you are always thinking of streamlining the system.

Adopting these mindset traits is the very necessary first step on your journey to embodying the Organizer Role.

Step 2: Choose an Activity to Practice the Role

This next section contains a range of activities designed to help you play the Organizer Role. Each activity aligns with the characteristics of the Organizer and will help you refine and internalize these traits.

If you play this role well, seek out activities or environments that stretch your skill. For example, you might be great at organizing at work but challenged by it at home, either by overplaying it or underplaying it. Or if you don't play this role well and value flying by the seat of your pants rather than planning ahead, give it a try. You may find that for many activities in your life, the Organizer Role offers needed, even if not wanted, structure.

For this role, choosing any activity offered below can take a while to practice. For example, if you begin with the first activity—setting clear, doable goals—you can include life goals, health goals, work goals, and many more. Think like an Organizer and practice setting and checking progress on your tracked and achievable goals.

Step 3: Repeat

Practicing these activities consistently will help these new mindset traits become second nature. The more you practice, the more adept you will become at embodying the Organizer Role. Remember, transformation doesn't happen overnight; be patient with yourself and stay committed to the process.

"Organizing is what you do before you do something so that when you do it, it is not all mixed up." -A. A. Milne

PRACTICAL EXERCISES: ORGANIZER

It's time to practice. Select activities that will help stretch and expand this role. If you want to approach this like the Organizer Role would, select an activity, consider how much time it will take and then put the activity on your calendar.

Set Clear Goals: Knowing what you want to achieve will give you a defined direction and a purpose to stay organized.

Judy, passionate about art journaling, decided to create a class sharing her skill with others. Knowing this required organization and SMART goals, she used her Organizer Role to create her plan. She defined her main objectives: teaching foundational techniques, creating a supportive community, and helping participants connect with their creative selves.

With her goals in place, Judy mapped out each session carefully, from beginner techniques to advanced exercises, ensuring each lesson built toward her objectives. She scheduled themes, created supply lists, and structured the course for a smooth flow.

Through her clear goals and careful organization, Judy's art journaling course became a supportive community, helping her students to both learn and connect in meaningful ways.

Prioritize Tasks: Not all tasks are created equal. Some are more important or more urgent than others. Learn to differentiate between high priority and low priority tasks. Prioritizing means choosing what deserves your time.

Tara was a schoolteacher overwhelmed by her many different projects: lesson planning, grading, parent-teacher meetings, and administrative paperwork. She decided to prioritize by impact and due dates. Grading assignments and lesson planning came first as they directly impacted her students' learning. Administrative work was next, and lastly, preparing for parent-teacher meetings she realized could wait until later in the month. By taking the time to plan and prioritize, she was able to manage her workload more effectively and reduce her stress.

Upgrade Time Management System: Assess your current system and make the necessary changes to keep track of your commitments and deadlines.

Diane, a busy lawyer, was always racing against time. Between court appearances, client meetings, and paperwork, she barely had a moment to spare. After learning about the Organizer Role, she considered how she used time. She was so good at "winging it," she had placed herself in constant reactionary mode.

She researched and found a suitable time management tool and began using it immediately. She blocked out specific times for court appearances and meetings, scheduled slots for focused paperwork, and even allocated time for breaks. Diane found that she was more efficient, less stressed, and even had time for a mind clearing walk during lunch.

Delegate: Recognize that you can't do everything yourself. If there are tasks that can be done by someone else, delegate them. In the personal realm, delegation includes asking for help.

Rachel, the head of a marketing team, was tasked with launching a new product. She tried to oversee every detail herself until she realized she was burning out and the work was suffering. Taking a step back, she decided that she needed to delegate.

She assigned market research to the team member with the strongest analytical skills, content creation to her most creative team member, and so forth. The product launch was a success, and Rachel found her team was more motivated and committed, having been entrusted with significant responsibilities.

Use Smart Tools and Technology: Make use of project management tools and industry specific software to help streamline processes and increase efficiency.

PLANNING THE ORGANIZER ROLE

Geanna is an executive assistant to a VP at a major tech company, where managing a packed schedule, high-priority projects, and constant communication is part of her daily routine. Juggling multiple moving parts was overwhelming—until she integrated smart productivity tools into her workflow.

She set up a centralized project management system, creating dedicated dashboards for key initiatives, tracking deadlines, and assigning follow-ups. Automated reminders ensured nothing slipped through the cracks, while collaboration tools helped streamline communication between departments.

By leveraging technology, Geanna transformed chaotic schedules into seamless operations. Now, she not only keeps everything on track but also anticipates needs, making her an indispensable strategic partner to her executive.

Break Down Large Tasks: Large tasks can seem overwhelming. Breaking them down into smaller, more manageable chunks can make them seem more achievable and less daunting.

When Erin was tasked with setting up a satellite office in her city, the project felt overwhelming. Finding a location, hiring staff, and getting everything up and running seemed like too much to tackle at once.

She took a deep breath and broke it down. First, she listed the essentials: an office space, basic furniture, internet, and a local support team. She set a deadline for each step and tackled them one by one.

Within days, she had a shortlist of office spaces. A week later, she secured a lease and ordered the necessary equipment. She hired a team, prioritizing key roles first. Instead of getting lost in the details, she focused on what mattered most—making steady progress.

By launch day, the office was fully functional, proving that even the biggest tasks become manageable when tackled step by step.

Evaluate Systems: Assess the effectiveness of your current systems and processes. Look for ways to improve or streamline them.

Diego worked in a mid-size manufacturing company that had been using the same production system for years. When production began to lag, Diego, using his Organizer Role mindset, evaluated their current system and identified bottlenecks and inefficiencies. He documented every slowdown, tracked workflow disruptions, and pinpointed outdated processes that were causing delays.

After compiling his findings, he presented a clear, data-driven report to management, outlining specific changes that could improve efficiency without disrupting operations. His recommendations included reorganizing workstations for better flow, updating scheduling methods, and streamlining inventory management.

Management implemented Diego's plan in phases, and within weeks, productivity showed measurable improvement. Downtime was reduced, orders were processed faster, and the team worked more smoothly. Diego's ability to break down a complex issue and create a structured solution not only increased production efficiency but also earned him recognition as a key problem-solver in the company.

Create a Structured Environment: Look around. Do you have a good system in place? Could it be better? Having an organized workspace can greatly increase productivity and creativity.

As a cinematographer, Leila thrived on precision and efficiency. Her workspace was well-structured, with cameras, lenses, and drives neatly stored. But as her projects grew in complexity, she needed a more advanced system to keep up.

Turning to her Organizer Role, she refined her workflow by creating dedicated zones for editing, color grading, and sound design. She streamlined her file management system, ensuring every project had a clear structure, and optimized her pre-production checklists to save time on set.

The impact was immediate. With a seamlessly organized process, Leila met tight deadlines with ease and had more mental space for creativity and storytelling. Organization wasn't just about order—it was the key to elevating her craft.

Make a Plan: Look out into your next few weeks or months. What would benefit from a more detailed plan? Try to anticipate potential issues or obstacles and create system to mitigate them.

Diana, a busy mother, found it challenging to manage her children's activities, household chores, and her part-time job. Every day felt like a juggling act, with last-minute scrambles and forgotten appointments adding unnecessary stress.

Determined to regain control, she learned about the Organizer Role and decided to plan her month in advance. She created a family calendar, mapping out school events, extracurricular activities, and work commitments. She allocated specific days and times for laundry, grocery shopping, and meal prep, ensuring that no task piled up unexpectedly.

To streamline her responsibilities further, she implemented small but effective systems—setting up reminders for bill payments, prepping meals on Sundays, and designating a drop zone for her children's school bags and supplies.

This advanced planning not only helped her manage time more effectively but also reduced the everyday chaos. With a clear plan in place, she felt less overwhelmed, more present with her family, and even found time to schedule in a massage—a luxury she hadn't enjoyed in years.

Diagnostic Assessment: Look at the systems you currently use. Are they working? What can you do to improve them? Regularly evaluate progress and adjust for performance.

Luca was the coach of sport team that had lost several games in a row. Frustrated but determined, he decided to step back and conduct a diagnostic assessment. As Peter Drucker famously said, "If you can't measure it, you can't improve it."

Taking this to heart, Luca reviewed game footage, analyzed player performance, and gathered feedback from the team. Patterns emerged—defensive gaps, missed scoring opportunities, and a lack of coordination in key moments. Armed with these insights, he adjusted their training approach, focusing on strengthening weak areas, refining strategies, and implementing targeted drills.

Over time, the team's cohesion improved, their confidence grew, and they turned their losing streak into a series of hard-earned victories.

Find and Remove Obstacles: What is always getting in your way? Identify and eliminate inefficiencies to streamline workflow.

Jasmine worked at a fast-paced tech firm, where innovation moved quickly—but approvals did not. She noticed that her team's progress was consistently hampered by a slow, cumbersome approval process for their designs. Delays piled up, projects stalled, and frustration grew.

Stepping into the Organizer Role, Jasmine took the initiative to diagnose the problem. She mapped out the approval workflow, identifying bottlenecks and redundant steps that added unnecessary delays. She then liaised with management to propose a more efficient system—one that reduced excessive back-and-forth, clarified decision-making authority, and introduced a streamlined digital approval tool.

The results were immediate. With a more agile process in place, her team could work more efficiently, iterate designs faster, and meet their deadlines without the usual roadblocks. By eliminating a persistent obstacle, Jasmine didn't just improve workflow—she empowered her team to focus on what they did best: creating cutting-edge solutions.

How Things Should Work: Create detailed process maps to ensure smooth operations. This visual tool aids in understanding and following the process efficiently.

Nia, a restaurant owner, noticed the kitchen operations were often chaotic during peak hours. She decided to create a detailed process flow for food preparation and delivery. This change improved the kitchen's efficiency, reduced order mix-ups, and improved customer satisfaction.

Communicate Effectively: Use clear, precise communication to avoid misunderstandings.

Arabelle, an office manager, often found that instructions were misunderstood, leading to mistakes that affected the team's productivity. Frustrated with the frequent errors, she decided to take a proactive approach to improve her communication. Recognizing that clarity was essential, she focussed on providing clear, concise instructions for every task and made it a point to confirm that her team understood them before moving on.

She implemented a brief check-in after each instruction session, encouraging her colleagues to ask questions and express any uncertainties. This small change drastically reduced errors and improved the office's overall efficiency. The team began to feel more empowered, and Arabelle noticed an increase in confidence as they tackled their tasks with greater clarity.

With fewer mistakes to correct, the atmosphere in the office became more positive and productive, fostering a culture of open communication and collaboration.

The key to mastering the Organizer Role is to continually strive for improvement. Even small changes can have a significant impact on your ability to organize and manage tasks effectively.

If you don't have a plan, you aren't playing the Organizer Role.

ADVANCED TIPS FOR PLAYING THE ORGANIZER ROLE

Mastering the Organizer Role isn't for the faint of heart. It's like easily juggling flaming torches while riding a unicycle on a tightrope.

If you can imagine that, you are thinking like the Organizer Role—coordinating different tasks while staying goal focused. It demands a combo of skills and a mindset that both creates and executes plans while always being ready to adapt to obstacles in the way.

To excel in this role, you need to equip yourself with a range of skills and tools, but two abilities stand head and shoulders above the rest:

- **Contingency Planning:** Developing the skill to foresee and manage the unexpected.
- **Mastering Delegation**: Engaging others to achieve together what can't be done alone.

In this chapter, we'll take an in-depth look at these two pivotal advanced skills and then close it out with a cautionary section on what happens when the Organizer Role is overplayed.

Contingency Planning: Planning for the Unexpected

When you play the Organizer Role, you're a pro at crafting and carrying out plans. But let's face it, life loves throwing curveballs. No matter how perfect your plans are, even the best-laid plans can sometimes go off-track due to life's unpredictable nature. When that happens, having a contingency plan in place makes all the difference in how things turn out.

What is Contingency Planning?

Simply put, contingency planning is your plan B. And maybe even your plan C, or D. The Organizer Role is constantly looking for potential potholes in the road ahead and figuring out how to avoid them.

These could be small disruptions, like getting sick or having to deal with surprise commitments. But it could also mean being prepared to tackle bigger challenges like emergency preparations for a natural disaster or planning an economic slump.

Whatever happens you're equipping yourself to handle it.

Why Waste Time with Contingency Planning?

You've got a plan and it's great, so why waste time dreaming up scenarios that might never happen? Here are three persuading perks to investing that extra time into alternate plans.

- The Ultimate Stress Buster: Life can be unpredictable, and let's face it, curveballs can be stressful. But with a solid contingency plan, you're prepped for the unexpected, reducing cortisol levels and keeping you cool, calm, and stress free.
- Hello, Better Plan B: Sometimes when you're working on a contingency plan, a strange thing happens. You stumble upon an alternative that's not just a fallback—it's actually better than Plan A.
- Better Safe Than Sorry: Imagine you're on a boat trip, but you didn't bother checking where the life vests were stashed. Suddenly, you hit rough waters and, well, you see where I'm going with this. If you've prepared for a potential situation (like a boat rocking more than you'd like), you'll be glad you have a plan ready to roll out. It's like that old saying goes, *"Prepare for the worst, hope for the best."*

So, before you dismiss contingency planning as a waste of precious time, consider the advantages. A modest investment in time and preparation can yield significant rewards, including reduced stress, unexpected improvements in systems, and enhanced readiness for life's inevitable surprises.

How to Create a Contingency Plan

Ready to create your contingency plan? Here's a simple step-by-step Organizer Role style guide:

1. Spot the Possible Hurdles: Look at your plans and figure out where things could potentially trip up. Are there any weak links? Could external factors, like bad weather, market fluctuations or people impact your plans?

2. Weigh the Risks: Not all bumps in the road are created equal. Some might just slow you down a bit, while others could bring your plans to a screeching halt. Think about the possible impact of each risk —will it cause delays? Additional costs? Affect others in your plan?

3. Prep Your Plan B (and C, and D): For each risk, come up with a backup strategy. This could be an alternate route to your goal, extra resources on standby, or even just some wiggle room in your timeline for dealing with unexpected delays.

4. Share the Plan: Make sure everyone involved in your plans knows about the contingency strategies. This ensures that if things do go sideways, everyone can quickly switch to the backup plan without panicking.

5. Keep Your Plans Fresh: Life changes, and so should your contingency plans. Regularly revisit and revise them to ensure they're up-to-date and ready to tackle whatever life has in store.

Contingency planning is not easy. It will take your planning skill to the next level. This ability to plan for the unexpected not only sets you apart with the Organizer Role, but also contributes significantly to the successful realization of the plans you, and others, make.

"Expect the best, plan for the worst, and prepare to be surprised." - Denis Waitley

Mastering Delegation: The Power of Empowering Others

Delegation is a critical skill tightly associated with all the roles but maybe most especially with the Organizer Role. This role is like being the conductor of a grand orchestra. You're leading the show, and you are not able to play all the instruments that are required. You need other people and other processes and other tools to all play their parts at the right time and in the right way, and that's where delegation—the art of assigning tasks—comes in.

If your goals are big, and let's face it, most tasks worth doing are, then you're going to need help to get it done. The Organizer Role is the planner and the delegator you need.

The What and Why of Delegation

Delegation, put simply, is the art of successful task distribution. It's not about dumping the work you don't want to do on someone else. Delegation is about making sure that the right tasks are in the right hands at the right time.

And yet, delegating might be a challenge for you. Maybe you don't like asking others for help. Maybe you don't like their work. Maybe you don't think they will help you. Maybe you think you should do it all. There are so many reasons why we avoid delegating so the first step is to get out of your own way. Delegation is necessary. Here are a few reasons:

- **You Get More Done:** When you delegate effectively, you're able to accomplish more in less time. That's because everyone is pitching in, doing what they do best.
- **Learning:** When tasks are delegated, more skills are combined. You and anyone involved gets a chance to learn from each other.
- **Building Connections:** Delegation can create a sense of unity. When everyone's got a part to play, everyone feels like they contribute to something bigger than themselves.

The How of Delegation

Knowing that you need to delegate is one thing. Being able to delegate effectively is another. Here are some key principles to keep in mind:

1. **Choosing the Right Tasks:** Delegation isn't about offloading tasks randomly. It's about looking at the tasks at hand and figuring out who or what tool can do them best.
2. **Choosing the Right People:** Assign tasks to people who either already have the skills to do them, or who have the potential to learn and benefit from them.
3. **Choosing the Right Tools:** Find tools that match your time, budget, and skill level. Finding the right tools might also be something that you need to delegate to someone else who is better at assessing what will fit the best.
4. **Communicate Clearly:** When you delegate, make sure the person knows exactly what's expected. Be clear about the outcome you're looking for, the timeline, and how much leeway they have in how they complete the task.
5. **Monitoring, Not Micromanaging:** Keep an eye on how things are going, but resist the urge to take over.

6. **Recognizing and Rewarding Effort:** As progress is made, celebrate advances along the way.

For the Organizer Role to truly excel, delegation is one of the most important skills you will need to master. Big jobs require help, either in appropriately placed tools or with well directed people.

In the next section we move on to the problems that arise when the Organizer Role is over used and tips to avoid this.

Avoiding the Pitfalls of Over Organizing

In any scenario—be it personal, familial, or professional—the Organizer Role is essential. This is the role that defines structure, focuses on productivity, and seeks efficiency. However, it's important to remember that too much of anything, including organization, can turn into a disadvantage. Overdoing it can complicate or even worsen situations rather than simplifying them. Here are some possible signs of the over-organizing.

Suppressed Creativity: Having a structure is necessary for success, but if it's overly rigid, it can prevent the free flow of innovative thoughts and ideas. When you over-manage every situation, it may inhibit the natural, creative responses that often lead to unique solutions.

Over-Dependence: Whether you're planning a family vacation or a professional project, if you're always making every decision, you could inadvertently create a reliance on your directives. This dependence could leave everyone stranded in your absence.

Overlooking Individual Strengths: In your quest to keep everything neatly arranged and smoothly running, you might assign tasks based only on what needs to be done, disregarding the unique abilities and preferences of those involved. This can lead to decreased motivation and subpar performance, whether it's at home or at work.

Cultivating Apathy or Worse: Constantly dictating what others should do and how they should do it might lead to discontent over time.

People generally prefer to feel like they're participating actively, rather than merely a minion following orders.

Striking the Right Balance

Avoiding the pitfall of over-organizing requires a delicate balance. Here are some pointers to keep in mind:

Encourage Independence: Whether it's a family member or a colleague, empower them to take charge of their tasks. This sense of autonomy will encourage initiative and shift responsibility from you to others.

Promote Open Communication: Make sure to create an environment where everyone involved feels comfortable voicing their ideas, opinions, and concerns. This strategy helps to make everyone feel valued and included.

Appreciate and Utilize Individual Strengths: Strive to understand the unique skills and strengths of each individual and assign tasks accordingly, whether it's choosing who will organize the family reunion or who will manage a work project.

Know When to Step Back: Not every situation calls for a stringent organizational approach. Learn to recognize when it's advantageous to step back and let things progress naturally. This can even lead to unexpected and beneficial outcomes.

As an Organizer, your role is critical, be it in personal, familial, or professional settings. However, it's important to remember that your ultimate goal is to facilitate a harmonious, productive, and empowering environment. Being a great Organizer is about expecting and preparing for the unexpected, boosting others to their best, and knowing when to pull back. It's tough, but when done right, it makes all the difference in the world in how plans unfold.

Blueprints For Success

The Organizer Role, unparalleled beyond compare,
In a world of chaos, they direct with care.
Amidst disarray, a calm they bestow,
Turning chaos to order, making everything flow.

Master of minutes, hours, and days,
Time bends to their will, in remarkable ways.
Advocate for plans, they chart the path ahead,
Ensuring resources are rightly spread.

Before action's taken, the blueprint's drawn,
To guide the steps from dusk to dawn.
From chores to tasks, to team goals scored,
They measure and plan for rewards to be stored.

Their calendars hum, their lists align,
They catch what slips through every time.
From tangled threads, they weave with grace,
Bringing calm and rhythm to every space.

In every endeavor, they hold the key,
To order, efficiency, and productivity.
So let us embrace, and fully extend,
The Organizer's virtues, on whom we depend.

SUMMARY

This chapter explored the role that specializes in creating order out of chaos. But playing the Organizer Role isn't only 'organizing'; it's planning ahead, structuring workflows, and eliminating inefficiency before it even has a chance to slow you down.

To put this into practice, let's summarize this chapter Organizer-style.

Project Goal: Summarize Organizer Role Chapter

◆ **Step 1: Define the Role**

🎯 **Objective:** Understand how Organizers bring clarity to complexity by creating systems. Learn about the importance of the role for designing structured processes. Recognize how this role can both save time and reduce stress.

◆ **Step 2: Consider the Impact of Playing (or Not Playing) the Organizer Role**

📖 **Example: Harvey's Story** – Through Harvey's experience, we examined how organization (or the lack of it) directly impacts outcomes. His story illustrates the power of planning ahead and the challenges that arise when structure is missing.

Later in the chapter, learn how Harvey changes his life direction by intentionally adopting this role more often.

◆ **Step 3: Develop the Organizer Mindset**

📓 **Key Focus Areas:**

- Strong planning skills—seeing the big picture while managing details
- Practice a mindset that values efficiency, order, and prioritization

- Reduce large projects into manageable, measurable, specified plans.
- Learn from examples of Organizer mindset thinking throughout the practice section.

◆ Step 4: Build & Test Your Own Systems

🛠 Action Steps:

- Create your own systems to keep things organized
- Break big tasks into achievable, even sharable, chunks
- Streamline processes to make work more efficient and repeatable

◆ Step 5: Identify & Overcome Challenges

⚠ Watch out for Roadblocks. Learn about different ways the Organizer Role can run into problems including:

- Over-planning instead of taking action
- Getting stuck in perfectionism
- Feeling overwhelmed by too much structure

✅ **Solution:** Adjust, simplify, and focus on progress over perfection. Partner with other roles is also a viable option for maximizing this role.

◆ Step 6: Execute & Refine

🛠 Action Steps. This role seeks to make things runs smoothly as well as increase in scope, efficiency and/or productivity. Two skills that are included that help with this include:

- Mastering Delegation – Consider and maybe even practice distributing tasks effectively while keeping big-picture control.

- Developing Contingency Planning – Anticipate potential obstacles and create backup plans to stay on track before you even get started.

🚀 **Final Takeaway:** Organizing isn't about control—it's about freedom. A well-structured system can give you more time, less stress, and greater focus on what truly matters.

📌 **Next Step: Make a Plan**

📝 What's one area you can organize right now that will make your life easier? For over achievers, make a list of all areas that need organization. That is your master list.

🎯 What systems do you need to create?

🔄 How will you track your progress?

Time to make a plan?

If you don't have a plan, you aren't playing the Organizer Role.

ONE QUICK TIP

One quick thing the reader could do to practice the Organizer Role is to make a plan for your day and your week. Set aside a few minutes and plan out what you want to get done the next seven days.

This is not a to-do list. It is the plan you will use to generate your to-do list. Focus on what you want to have accomplished. Imagine the finished project and create the overall plan that is needed to get you there. This plan is what you will use to create your Implementor style to-do list.

The Organizer Role sees what the end looks like and develops a plan to get there. Try it!

"Life truly begins when you put your house in order."
-Marie Kondo

CLARITY FROM AN ORGANIZER

The moment I learned about the Organizer Role, I knew it was my top role. I live for a good plan!

Life is complicated, with my job, family activities, and my own personal needs. The Organizer Role describes how I sort and order life's jumbled task pile to put everything precisely where it belongs.

There is something incredibly satisfying about bringing order to chaos. Whether it's arranging a cluttered workspace, planning a quarterly project at work, or sorting out my family's weekly schedule, I take on what looks like an impossible mess and turn it into…order!

The thrill of optimizing? It's unbeatable. Faster, better, more, easier are all words I like. If I can unravel a convoluted process, or streamline a bulky system, the reward I get is a sigh of relief. Nothing compares. It's a pat on the back, a nod of gratitude, and it's what keeps me going.

The Organizer Role isn't just about organizing things or tasks. It's also how I look at my time. I know exactly how much time I have which helps me to know what to add to my schedule. Or maybe more importantly, when to say no when I simply have no more time. It's taught me to pace myself, to sketch out schedules that are ambitious yet achievable.

But what truly sets this role apart for me is balance. It's not all work and no play. It's penciling in that spa day, family game night, or just some "me time." Having a plan at work is necessary but having a plan at home is life changing.

To me, playing the Organizer Role is so much more than planning and organizing—it's about living a life that is productive, balanced, and intentional. This is definitely my most useful role!

LIVING OUT THE LUMINARY ROLE
LIVING OUTLOUD

Are you engaging and inspiring?
Do you have an optimistic and enthusiastic outlook?
Are you a communicator, able to energize others?
Do you know a lot of people and keep in touch
with most of them?
This is the LUMINARY ROLE!

THE CURTAIN RISES, the spotlight is yours—this is the starring role. The Luminary Role is all about captivating, inspiring, and rallying others around connections, ideas, or activities. And just like a true performer, those who play this role well earn their standing ovation.

This section introduces the crucial function of the Luminary Role, breaking down the attributes and behaviors that make it so compelling. Whether you naturally thrive in this role or shy away from it, you'll find practical guidance to help you strengthen your ability to step into the spotlight with confidence.

For those unsure about embracing the Luminary Role, we'll explore why it matters and how it can help you—whether in leadership, relationships, or personal growth. The goal is to develop all Seven Roles, and if this is one you tend to avoid, this section might just change your mind.

Of course, no role is without its challenges. Playing the Luminary Role too much or at the wrong time can create obstacles, so we'll also cover advanced skills to help you refine and master this role at a higher level.

This is the get-out-in-front, be-bold, speak-up-and-spark-inspiration role. And the first trait you need? Confidence.

You can do this.

Like a Luminary.

Story Part 1: Lois

[Lois: A 40 something analyst.] I work as data analyst in a large corporation. My job offers me safety—I like both routine and predictability. I arrive at work every day at eight, immerse myself in spreadsheets and databases, attend a few meetings, and then head home by five. I am good at interpreting data, but my work seldom opens doors for interpersonal engagement or creative expression.

Away from work, I enjoy a small group of close friends I have known for many years. I like reading or taking long walks on the weekends but recently I have begun to wonder if I am stuck in a rut. I feel like I am missing a deeper connection with the greater world around me. Then I heard about the Luminary Role and realized not only do I not play that role much, I am not sure I play it at all.

Don't get me wrong. I am not unhappy with who I am. I just can't ignore the sense that there is something more, something different I could and should be exploring. I want to put more into my life. I want to get more out of my life.

Sometimes, like Lois, we make role changes because we know there is or could be more to our lives. The roles offer new behaviors which can open new doors.

HOW CAN THE LUMINARY ROLE HELP YOU?

Imagine walking into a room possessing the courage to approach unfamiliar people and the verbal nimbleness to initiate dialogue and create connections. Imagine having the ability to speak out boldly, not from a place of flamboyant extroversion, but from a profound sense of self, and the knowledge that every voice, including yours, has value. This is the essence of the Luminary Role. It's not about being the loudest in the room but about having the audacity to be authentically you, fearlessly inviting others into your world and easily stepping into theirs.

The Luminary Role is about being both self-focused and other-focused at the same time in order to make connections that matter. It's about not waiting for the world to notice you but reaching out and making the first move.

Perhaps you're thinking, "this doesn't sound like me." Maybe you're more reserved, preferring to stay in the background rather than taking center stage. And that's okay. Every individual has their unique strengths. But what if you could tap into just a fraction of the Luminary Role's appeal? What if, by understanding and adopting some of their traits, you could enhance your own interpersonal skills and your potential for influencing others?

If you often find yourself shying away from social settings, or if you feel like your ideas aren't being well-received, learning from the Luminary Role could be the key to unlocking a new level of confidence and influence in group dynamics. Even if you don't consider yourself an extrovert, embracing aspects of this role can open doors to new friendships, leadership opportunities, and a richer, more connected experience in any setting.

Or, perhaps this is one of your role strengths. Learning more about it can take your role play to the next level, first by recognizing, appreciating and investing more in the valuable traits of this role and second by learning how to better locate and manage its weaknesses.

Regardless, the Luminary Role focuses the spotlight on you, leveraging your capacity to stand out, make an impression on the world and ultimately, be memorable.

IF YOU PLAY THE LUMINARY ROLE

The Luminary Role welcomes and even encourages attention. If you are feeling sidelined, this is the role that can fix that. There is no forgetting someone who plays the Luminary Role.

Charisma Connector: You establish more relationships through your outgoing and charismatic nature.

Positivity Magnet: Your positivity attracts and inspires others, fostering strong social connections.

Natural Leader: You find it easier to lead in various contexts, given your ability and desire to stand up and stand out.

Workplace Motivator: Your career benefits from being inspirational at work.

Experience Seeker: Your personal life becomes more diverse and fulfilling, as you seek out and embrace new experiences.

Confidence Exemplar: Your self-confidence improves. "I can" is a Luminary phrase.

Vision Ignitor: You inspire and motivate others. You bring genuine contagious excitement to pretty much anything.

Momentum Infuser: The extra energy the Luminary Role brings acts like a breath of fresh air to a goal or group. This can enhance, and even initiate, momentum.

Communication Maestro: You possess strong, well-practiced communication skills.

Network Broker: You have a lot of contacts. You enjoy maintaining your extensive network and are a conduit for connecting people.

Let's see what happens when Lois incorporates the Luminary Role in her life.

Story Part 2: Lois

The very first day I decided to play more of the Luminary Role, I felt the difference. I felt more confident. Confidence is a choice? I don't know, but whatever it was, I felt different. Before I even spoke up, I felt like I had given myself permission to change and that changed what I did and what I said and even how I said it.

At work, I started voicing my opinions and ideas during meetings. Then I began to engage my colleagues in conversations, breaking my well earned reputation of being a reserved person. At first, it felt awkward and there were a few stumbles along the way but instead of letting that derail me, I used it to learn and improve my conversational abilities. It wasn't long before I noticed a change—my interactions were richer, and I felt a stronger sense of connection and a feeling of contribution. It wasn't about being perfect. It was about being seen. I felt more valued.

I made a conscious decision to think like a leader. This meant viewing work from the perspective of the greater team, with an eye on corporate goals. I helped others achieve necessary goals. I mentored new hires. I volunteered rather than waiting to be asked. This change in perspective not only transformed my work dynamics but was also recognized by my superiors. It was humbling to learn that I was now being considered as a potential leader within the company.

Personally, I sought to expand my social network too. One key aspect of the Luminary Role that I wanted to cultivate was spontaneity. So, I said yes to new experiences. Instead of spending quiet weekends alone which truthfully, I love, I explored different parts of my city. I embraced the challenge of making new friends by starting up conversations. I tried different hobbies, attending group meetings to meet people that enjoy the same things. It wasn't always easy, but every new experience brought me one step closer to embodying the Luminary

Role. I felt more bold, more capable, and a growing confidence I hadn't felt before. Life didn't seem so scary.

Most importantly, my personal life flourished. I found myself at the heart of a bustling social network, sometimes even acting as a bridge between different groups of friends. The deep satisfaction I got from these connections was a testament to the power of the Luminary Role. I was no longer just another face in the crowd—I had become someone people wanted to be around.

Embracing the Luminary Role wasn't about becoming someone else for Lois. Instead, it was about allowing herself to be seen, to shine brighter, to be more open and engaging, to influence and inspire others. The difference it made was profound.

THE LUMINARY ROLE BULLETED

*Inspire with engagement, lead with boldness,
pursue with enthusiasm.*

Enthusiastic Communicator: They communicate their enthusiasm to others, inspiring and motivating them.

Inspirational: Luminaries are skilled at building momentum around a shared vision.

Effective Storyteller: They use engaging, interesting, and relevant stories to communicate effectively.

Network Builder: They maintain a wide network both personally and professionally.

People Oriented: This role enjoys being around people and engaging in conversations.

Center of Attention: They are comfortable with, value and even seek to be the center of attention.

Opinionated: They are not timid about speaking up and sharing their thoughts and opinions.

Natural Leaders: They naturally take up leadership roles even if only informally. They draw people towards them with their charisma or passion.

Adaptable and Spontaneous: They exhibit adaptability and spontaneity, welcoming and responding quickly to unexpected opportunities and experiences.

Relationship Broker: They are adept and helpful at fostering connections between others, further expanding and deepening their relational network.

If this role is unused or underdeveloped:

- Maintains relationships that should be terminated.
- Waits for others to initiate relationship.
- Slow to speak or share, timid.

If this role is overused:

- Mobilize people but with unclear vision or purpose.
- Exhaust network.
- Poor listening/too much talking

THE LUMINARY ROLE DESCRIBED

The Luminary Role is the message bearer, passionate connector, and inspiring enthusiast. Dynamic, engaging, and effortlessly inclusive, this role naturally attracts attention, drawing others toward a project, group or idea.

Research identifies four qualities essential to
leadership: intelligence, sensitivity, dedication, and dynamism. While many people possess intelligence, sensitivity, and dedication, it is dynamism—a vibrant energy filled with enthusiasm and inclusivity—that sets the Luminary apart. Dynamism not only captivates interest but also replaces indifference with genuine excitement. People often label Luminaries as "natural-born leaders," yet this leadership comes from actively embracing and expressing their Luminary Role.

Central to the Luminary Role is a practiced commitment to maintain connections. This includes regular check ins and scheduled meetups. Relationships, for Luminaries, are sources of both immediate genuine pleasure and for the opportunity to create even more relationships.

But the Luminary's influence extends far beyond simply attracting others to their growing network of people. They actively seek opportunities to facilitate connections. Luminaries take pride in referring and introducing people, enjoying their role as catalysts who spark positive changes in individuals and communities through their extensive network.

Gifted communicators, Luminaries don't wait to start up a conversation and always have something to say. They excel in storytelling. Advanced Luminaries can craft engaging stories from virtually any topic, a skill highly valued, especially in impromptu speaking situations.

Thanks to their exceptional social confidence and communicative skill, Luminaries are rarely confined to specific groups or social circles. They feel implicitly invited to participate wherever they are, including stepping into the spotlight with ease. Indeed, this role is made for settings that require public speaking. Those who play this role are drawn to platforms where they can openly share ideas *and* energy.

When faced with pressures or challenges, Luminaries exhibit a resilient resolve. Deadlines, unfavorable news, obstacles, and rejection become fuel that ignites their determination, reinforcing their boldness. Their inherent bravery and fearless enthusiasm enable them to face and overcome difficulties with remarkable optimism.

Ultimately, the Luminary Role combines bold enthusiasm, engaging communication, and a 'happy to step in the spotlight' attitude. This magnetic combination draws others in, creating an environment where everyone feels energized, included, and motivated.

"Nothing great was ever achieved without enthusiasm."
— Ralph Waldo Emerson

LUMINARY ROLE PRACTICED

This section offers practical activities with examples to help you practice the Luminary Role. The journey to embody this role involves three steps, starting with the most crucial: adopting the Luminary mindset.

A mindset description for this role is challenging to define because it's more about choosing to project yourself. The following steps are ideas on how to be more bold: be seen, be heard. This is the role that ensures your message and presence are unforgettable.

Step 1: Adopt the Mindset of the Luminary Role

To truly embody the Luminary Role, you need to adopt a mindset characterized by energy and enthusiasm. Here are some ways to connect with this role.

Enthusiastic Connector: You enjoy sharing your excitement with others.

Inspirational: You aim to engage and motivate.

Delightful Storyteller: You tell stories that captivate the audience.

Socially Extraverted: You build and nurture relational networks.

Spotlight Seeker: You are comfortable being the center of attention.

Outspoken: You are confident about sharing your thoughts and opinions.

Some of the other roles have mindsets that are a bit easier to adapt to and use than the Luminary Role. That is because this role requires the extraversion trait, which is challenging for those who tend to be more introverted. If that is you, practicing any one of the mindset suggestions above might be a good first step.

Remember, your role is not you. It is a tool to help you achieve the goals you are striving for. Thinking and then behaving like the Luminary is a role you choose to play.

Step 2: Choose an Activity to Practice the Role

You may decide to practice putting on the Luminary Role mindset over a week or a month. You will know you are making progress if you start to more easily feel confident and bold. The next section contains a range of activities designed to help you practice. Each activity aligns with the characteristics of the Luminary Role and will assist you in refining and internalizing these traits. As with all the role practice suggestions, the activities you don't want to do are likely the ones that you need most.

Step 3: Repeat

Practicing these activities consistently will enable these new mindset traits to become second nature. The more you practice, the more adept you will become at embodying the Luminary Role. The goal is not to become an extravert, the goal is to know how to act like one when you need to.

PRACTICAL EXERCISES: LUMINARY

This is the practice section for the Luminary Role. If you want to build up this role, read through this section and choose an activity that will stretch you. All the roles can be improved, so no matter how well or how poorly you play a role, you can increase your ability. If you want to act like a Luminary, choose the one that makes you most uncomfortable and then do that one with great enthusiasm.

Take the Fear Out of Speaking: Practice and improve your communication skills. Join a public speaking club like Toastmasters or simply begin by speaking up. The idea is to get comfortable with expressing your ideas in front of a group.

Michelle has always been a bit reserved when it comes to public speaking. However, she decided to join her local speech club to over-

come this hurdle. Week by week, Michelle stands up, delivers speeches and receives constructive feedback from the members. Over time, she became more comfortable with public speaking, her delivery improved, and she even started to enjoy it. Michelle's improved communication skills were recognized at her workplace, and she seized the opportunity to present the quarterly business review in front of her entire team when it was offered.

Contagious Enthusiasm: Share your enthusiasm in a relationship, toward a goal, or at an event.

Moose is the coffee shop barista we all want to see first thing every morning. Each day, she greets every customer who walks in the door with a warm smile and a cheerful "How can I brighten your day?" She remembers regulars' favorite orders and suggests new drinks to more adventurous souls.

One morning, a weary customer enters, visibly stressed. Moose immediately senses their mood and offers a comforting recommendation for a rich mocha. The customer's face brightens with the recognition and feeling of being seen.

Her positivity is contagious. The more she shares that upbeat energy, the more it becomes the atmosphere of the entire coffee shop. Regulars gather, exchanging stories and laughter, inspired by her enthusiasm. As a result, what could be just another routine morning becomes a vibrant community experience.

Through her unwavering positivity, Moose reminds us that a little enthusiasm can go a long way, transforming not just individual experiences but the collective spirit of the space.

Network Building: Attend a networking event, either virtually or in-person, and aim to have meaningful conversations with at least five new people. Try to focus on engaging them and discovering where you might connect them with others in your network.

Ethan is a freelance graphic designer who wanted to expand his network to grow his client base. He attended a virtual networking event in his industry. At the event, Ethan intentionally started up conversations with as many people as he could. He adopted the mindset of the initiator, not the bystander. He showed enthusiastic interest in whatever their work was and then shared what he was doing.

By the end of the event, he had successfully made connections with several potential clients and even received a few project inquiries. Surprisingly, he also found that he enjoyed it.

Personal Storytelling: Create and share a personal story that highlights your passion, experiences, or interests. This could be a social media post, a blog, or a speech at a public gathering. Notice the reactions and feedback you receive and adjust your approach accordingly.

Madeleine loves retro games and decides to create a Twitch account to share her passion. Excited yet nervous, she prepares for her first live stream, envisioning a community centered around nostalgia.

During her inaugural stream, she plays classic games like Super Mario Bros. and while sharing her memories of game play. The chat quickly fills with comments from fellow retro enthusiasts, creating an immediate sense of connection.

Encouraged by the positive feedback, Madeleine refines her approach, introducing themed nights and inviting viewers to play specific games together. She balances storytelling with engaging gameplay commentary, making her streams both inspiring and entertaining.

Curating Connections: Try to connect two people in your network who could mutually benefit from knowing each other. Explain to each why you think they should connect, highlighting the potential benefits for both.

Meaghan enjoys bringing people together. Her networking skills shine in her Luminary Role, where she looks for opportunities to create meaningful connections.

One day, she realizes that her friend Anaya, a small business owner, could benefit from meeting Gabriel, a financial advisor with experience helping startups. Instead of a casual introduction, Meaghan reaches out to each of them individually. She highlights Gabriel's expertise to Anaya, explaining how his insights could help her business grow. To Gabriel, she shares Anaya's vision and how her network might open new opportunities for him.

By the time they connect, they already see the value in working together.

Thanks to Meaghan's Luminary approach, a meaningful collaboration begins—one that benefits them both and reinforces her skill at creating purposeful connections.

Embrace Challenges: Pick a challenging goal that stretches you outside of your comfort zone. Share this goal with others, describing why it's important to you and how you plan to achieve it, inspiring others with your resolve and enthusiasm.

Pick a challenging goal that stretches you outside of your comfort zone. Share this goal with others, describing why it's important to you and how you plan to achieve it, inspiring others with your resolve and enthusiasm.

Daniel, an ambitious software developer, had always dreamed of building his own mobile app. But the task felt overwhelming—too many unknowns, too many reasons to put it off. However, after learning about the Luminary Role, he recognized that bold action and shared vision could help him move forward.

Instead of working in isolation, Daniel embraced the Luminary trait of inspiring others and openly shared his goal. He explained his vision to friends and mentors, outlining why the app mattered and the steps he planned to take. His enthusiasm was contagious. Encouraged by their support, he gained not just valuable advice, but a network of people invested in his success.

In the process, Daniel built more than just an app—he built momentum. His willingness to share his vision and invite others into the journey transformed his challenge into a collaborative effort, reinforcing the power of the Luminary Role in bringing ideas to life.

Exude Positivity: Practice maintaining a positive attitude even when faced with challenges or negativity.

Bryan is known for his unwavering optimism, a trait that fuels his business growth. As he focuses on expanding through networking, he approaches each connection with enthusiasm and purpose.

When a business setback arises, frustration would be easy—but Bryan chooses a different path. He sees challenges as opportunities to build resilience, leaning into his optimism and trusting that each effort moves him closer to success.

His positivity is infectious, strengthening both new and existing relationships. By maintaining a confident, forward-thinking mindset, Bryan not only propels his business but also inspires those around him, creating a ripple effect of encouragement and opportunity.

Improv Classes: Joining an improv class can enhance your spontaneity, creativity, and adaptability, while also honing your storytelling and public speaking skills. Improv often involves working as part of a team and quick, dynamic responses—all crucial to the Luminary Role.

Leonard, an aspiring public speaker, recognized the Luminary Role's potential to elevate his skills. To cultivate his spontaneity, creativity, and adaptability, he joined an improv class. The class was filled with unexpected scenarios that forced him to think on his feet, connect with others in a dynamic way, and develop engaging stories on the spot.

This not only improved his public speaking skills but also helped him become more comfortable with unpredictability, an essential trait for anyone embodying the Luminary Role. His newfound skills made his *speeches more engaging enabling him to convey his messages more effectively.*

Charismatic Leadership Exercise: Lead a group activity, like a team-building exercise at work, a community volunteering event, or a sports team. Focus on inspiring others and creating an inclusive and engaging environment.

Bri, an interpreter for the Deaf community, was asked to organize a birthday party with a mixed group of Deaf and hearing children. Wanting something lively and inclusive, she planned a visual scavenger hunt—using sign language clues, visual puzzles, and collaborative challenges to make sure every child could join in.

Before the game began, Bri explained the rules in clear, expressive ASL and ensured that hearing participants had access to interpretation. During the activity, she didn't just observe—she joined in, encouraged the kids, and helped them connect and collaborate across language and communication styles. Her creativity and warmth set the tone for celebration and inclusion.

By the end of the party, it wasn't about who found the most clues. It was about laughter, belonging, and the joy of playing together.

"Be genuine. Be remarkable. Be worth connecting with." -Seth Godin

---

ADVANCED TIPS FOR PLAYING THE LUMINARY ROLE

Playing the Luminary can be fun and energizing, but it is not without challenges. It is a very social role, so if you seek to master it, it might expose any inclusion/exclusion triggers that you have, including the fear of missing out (FOMO). Another challenge might arise because of its front and center type of sociability which can look like a power play for influence.

Here are suggestions for how to grow this role to mastery without feeling FOMO or being accused of making power plays.

I Can't Be Everywhere?!

The Luminary Role, with its characteristic energy, enthusiasm, and engagement runs the risk of experiencing the Fear of Missing Out (FOMO). Given this role's natural inclination to connect with others, stay informed, and be at the center of happenings, the Luminary Role can find it challenging to accept that they can't be everywhere at once or involved in every project, event, or conversation. This can lead to anxiety, dissatisfaction, and even burnout if not properly addressed or managed.

The first step in combating FOMO is acknowledging it. If the goal of the Luminary Role is to actively seek engagement with others, it will include choosing which activities you have time for and saying no to the rest. FOMO is a natural consequence of calendar pruning. But in our highly connected world, it is too easy to see what we are missing out on. The sensation of missing an opportunity, event, or conversation is perfectly normal, but it's important to remember that no one can be everywhere at once.

Here are some strategies that those who play the Luminary Role can employ to overcome FOMO.

Prioritization: If you choose to play this role, you need to take time to consider your goals, responsibilities, and passions, and prioritize accordingly. Not every event or discussion will align with your objectives. By focusing on what truly matters to you, you can ensure you are spending your time and energy in the places where you can make the most impact.

Set Boundaries: Given this role's powerful ability to connect with others, the Luminary Role may find it difficult to say no when connection is the call. However, setting boundaries is crucial. This might involve limiting the time spent on social media, or saying no to certain invitations or requests, enabling you to focus on your most valued activities and relationships.

Quality over Quantity: Those who play this role should remember that it's often the meaningful and impactful connections that carry more weight than numerous superficial ones. Focusing on deepening existing relationships can be more rewarding and beneficial than constantly trying to form new ones.

Time for Solitude: While the Luminary Role is naturally inclined towards social activities, it is important, even vital, to carve out quiet time. This alone time is critical for recharging, reflecting and ultimately to be able to maintain enthusiasm and positivity. Whether it's taking a quiet walk, reading a book, or just sitting in solitude, these moments of peace can help you rejuvenate and reset as to not grow weary of public time.

Celebrate Achievements: Regularly reflecting on and celebrating personal accomplishments can foster a greater sense of self-appreciation and contentment. This helps to reduce the urge to negatively compare yourself with others or feel like they're missing out.

By using these strategies, your Luminary Role can effectively manage FOMO and continue to thrive. The key is not to be everywhere at once, but to make a significant and positive impact everywhere you choose to be.

Let's move on to the next advanced tip for playing this role: how to handle kickback from others.

Power Play

The Luminary Role, with its boundless charisma and penchant for drawing attention, can sometimes be misconstrued by others as engaging in power plays. While the luminous enthusiasm and engaging demeanor of this role can serve as an attractant for others, certain aspects of their behavior might be perceived as overbearing, causing discomfort among peers or colleagues.

People who play the Luminary Role often have a whole treasure trove of ideas, stories, and projects that they're super excited about and can't wait to share. But there's a fine line between getting people excited about something and overwhelming them. Sometimes, in their eagerness to share everything they're passionate about it can feel like a deluge of information that leaves others feeling a bit drenched and verbally overwhelmed.

Moreover, if the Luminary Role is overplayed, it may lead to dominating conversations. This dominance can unintentionally silence others or suppress their ability to contribute to the discussion. Even though the intention of this role is to generate enthusiasm and stimulate conversation, it can sometimes come across as monopolizing the dialogue.

And finally, a Luminary's social confidence and boldness can be perceived as showboating. This role is at ease being the center of attention, and this can be interpreted by some as an attempt to steal the limelight or exert power.

While these challenges are inherent to the dynamics of anyone who plays the very public-facing Luminary Role, they can sometimes cast a shadow over the role's many positive attributes, such as its ability to inspire others, spread optimism, and be a catalyst for change.

Here are three simple tips to avoid these stumblers:

1. While it's natural for the Luminary Role to be enthusiastic and share their ideas, it's crucial to ensure that conversations are a two-way street. Actively listening to others not only demonstrates respect but can also provide you new perspectives.
2. The Luminary Role draws from a wealth of experiences and insights to share stories. But don't forget to tailor your stories to your audience, creating a mutually enriching experience. It's a subtle art, and one worth developing.
3. The Luminary Role is about being seen and being heard. If you master it, use that gift to illuminate others as well. Invite them to share their ideas and perspectives, creating an atmosphere of collaborative brilliance. It's a joy to see the spark in others that you have kindled. Remember, a master Luminary creates more Luminaries.

Mastering the Luminary Role should be and can be exciting. After all, the goal is to share excitement and enthusiasm with others.

Just watch out for FOMO and overstepping others with your boldness and…enjoy the spotlight!

"You were born to stand out, not to fit in." — Roy T. Bennett

Curtain Calls!

In the grand play of life, who shines so bright?
It's the Luminary, and oh what a sight!
They talk, they laugh, their joy takes flight,
In their glow, the world seems to just feel right.

They're the talk of the town, with stories to tell,
At parties, at meetings, they ring the bell.
A dash of charisma, a sprinkle of swell,
In their company, all worries quell.

Hey there, friend, join their exciting game,
In their world, no two days are the same.
With infectious enthusiasm, they proclaim,
"Life's too short for boredom's claim!"

They enter a room, and the dullness departs,
With sparkle in speech and warmth in their hearts.
With laughter and flair, and a few clever tricks,
The Luminary's magic? It simply sticks.

They connect, they inspire, they create,
Breaking boundaries, opening the gate.
Luminary Role? Oh, it's absolutely great,
Jump in, and let's illuminate!

SUMMARY

The Luminary Role isn't only openly stepping into the spotlight—it's also drawing others in, igniting excitement, and creating momentum. If you've ever felt the thrill of inspiring others, rallying a group, or delivering a message that truly landed, you've tapped into the power of the Luminary Role.

This is the rallying role. When a cause needs a champion, when a movement needs momentum, when a room needs energy—the Luminary steps up. This role isn't just magnetic; it's electric.

In this chapter, we explored what makes this role so powerful and why charisma, communication, and connection are its key strengths. Some of the areas covered included:

Practicing the Role – You worked through exercises designed to help you own the room, tell compelling stories, expand your network, and develop stage presence—whether that stage is a conference, a meeting, or a conversation with friends.

Stepping into Leadership – The Luminary Role says YES when asked to step forward. But leadership in this role isn't about control—it's about inspiration, encouragement, and sparking action in others.

Beyond the Spotlight – The Luminary Role is not attention for attention's sake. It's about using your voice, presence and content to create lasting impact. Impact isn't about being seen—it's about being remembered.

What's Next? Your Call to Action!

- Are you letting your voice be heard?
- Are you showing up with confidence, or holding back?
- Who could you inspire today?

Speak up. Step forward. Spark something. Engage the Luminary Role, and let your light shine.

Being seen is momentary. Being remembered matters.

ONE QUICK TIP

The Luminary Role connects! If you want to strengthen this role, reach out right now to someone.

To start practicing the Luminary Role is to proactively engage in conversations with others, be it in a professional setting, a social gathering, in the elevator or the grocery store, or at home with friends and family. Practice reaching out and engaging with others.

This simple act of initiating and maintaining appealing conversations with others will help cultivate the core traits of a Luminary, including charisma, extraversion, and the ability to connect and inspire others.

HELLO FROM A LUMINARY

Hello there, my friends!

What's awesome about being a Luminary, you ask? Oh, where do I even start!

As a Luminary, I get to inspire and influence people. I can't emphasize enough the exhilarating feeling that comes with it. Imagine helping someone find their passion or encouraging them to take that one daring step that completely transforms their life. I get to experience that almost every day. I'm a catalyst for change, but not just any change: the kind that makes a real, positive difference.

Now, I don't mean to say that playing the Luminary Role means you have to be the life of every party (although it's a bonus if you are!). You see, at the heart of this is the desire to connect with others and inspire them. It's about being passionate about what you do and sharing that enthusiasm with others. It's about making everyone around you feel valued and included, whether it's in a conversation, a project, or even a casual chat.

There's no denying that the Luminary Role requires a fair bit of extraversion. You need to be able to initiate conversations, be open to meeting new people, and enjoy the process of engaging with others. But hey, don't worry if you're not there yet. It's a journey, and like any journey, it takes time and practice.

I know it sounds like a lot. But trust me, as you start practicing this role, it gets easier, and more importantly, it becomes incredibly rewarding. You'll find a newfound confidence in your ability to handle social situations and inspire others. And you will have as many activities on your schedule as you want! Want the first step? Say hello first!

So, I'm encouraging all of you to give the Luminary Role a shot. Don't be afraid to step up and be seen. It's a role that's not just about you, but also about making a real impact on those around you.

APPRECIATING THE INVESTOR ROLE
LIVING SUBSTANTIALLY

Are you strategic and value-driven in your decision-making?
Do you evaluate potential outcomes and risks?
Are you inclusive and seek out diverse perspectives?
Do you focus on achieving your desired outcomes and making a difference?
This is the INVESTOR ROLE!

WELCOME to the very valuable chapter on the Investor Role. This is likely the most polarized role—people either love it or hate it. For those who hate it, the assumption is that it is about a love for money, but that is not true. This role simply does not fear, avoid, or reject the value of investing.

And the best investments aren't always financial. Playing the Investor Role well means managing your time, energy, and relationships with the same level of strategic foresight as financial assets. It's about choosing where to allocate resources, weighing risks and opportunities, and ensuring that every decision leads to meaningful outcomes—whether in your career, your personal growth, or your future.

And perhaps most importantly, the Investor Role defines generosity. Excellent Investors don't just accumulate—they give. They invest in people, causes, and ideas, knowing that the greatest impact comes from what is shared.

This chapter provides a detailed breakdown of what it means to play the Investor Role effectively. We'll explore the key attributes of this role, followed by actionable strategies and practice tips to refine your decision-making. As with all the roles, you'll see real-life examples illustrating the Investor Role in action.

Along the way, we'll highlight the lasting benefits of embracing this role—including greater personal and professional advancement, stronger results from your efforts, and yes, financial stability.

Whether you naturally lean into the Investor Role or find it a challenge to play, this chapter will help you sharpen your ability to think strategically, invest wisely, and maximize your influence. The goal is to help you understand the abundant potential of the Investor Role—and start seeing results in every area of life.

Let's look at what life looks like when this role is underutilized.

Story Part 1: Fiona

[Fiona: a 50 something first generation immigrant.] Fiona is an engaging and determined woman who owns a quaint bakery in the heart of a bustling city. Everyone adores her pastries, and her bakery has a charm that big-name chains lack. But for all its popularity and potential, Fiona's bakery is just scraping by. At first glance, it looks like an unfortunate twist of fate, but those in the know can tell that Fiona is missing a crucial element in her approach to business—the Investor Role.

Fiona is a genius in the kitchen. She has a passion for baking, creating the most delicious and aesthetically pleasing pastries you can find in the city. But her relationship with money is, to put it mildly, uncomfortable. She recoils at the mention of budgets, financial reports, and profit margins. These terms are like a foreign language to her, and she operates her business mostly on hope and goodwill, rather than on sound financial planning.

Fiona appreciates quality but not necessarily value. She frequently overspends on high-end ingredients and pays premium prices for services, resulting in her resources quickly draining away. She lacks the negotiation skills needed to secure better deals from her suppliers, and her financial naivety means she hardly notices the heavy toll this takes on her finances.

Fiona's professional network is also stagnant. She is surrounded by the same people, not because they are contributing to her business's growth but simply because they have always been there. She fails to recognize the potential benefits of networking and misses out on opportunities for business collaborations.

Fiona's six employees are a loyal, talented and dedicated bunch, but they are frustrated. They see the potential in the bakery and want to see it flourish. However, Fiona's avoidance of financial matters and her focus on perfecting pastries over profitability undermine the business's overall success. As much as they like her and the work they do at the bakery, they keep a watch on the job market just in case.

Eventually, it becomes painfully clear that Fiona's reluctance to embrace the Investor Role is leading her beloved bakery down a path of downward financial struggle. By avoiding dealing with money, she is creating a cycle of financial mismanagement and increasing inefficiency. Her lack of focus on profitability and her inability to manage her resources strategically has placed her business at risk.

"An investor without investment objectives is like a traveler without a destination." — Ralph Seger

---

HOW CAN THE INVESTOR ROLE HELP YOU?

Playing the Investor Role is very impactful on all areas of life, from personal to professional to interpersonal or relational.

In relationships: The Investor Role can foster stronger and more productive connections. It helps to identify individuals in your network who are likely to provide valuable insights, useful collaboration, or needed support. Moreover, those who play the Investor Role are valued as trusted partners. If the goal is to create usable results, it is easy to see how being successful at this would create mutually beneficial partnerships.

In your career: In a professional setting, playing the Investor Role equips you to handle projects more economically, making you an asset to a team or organization. This role focuses on optimizing resources, identifying opportunities, and steering projects or tasks towards greater profitability. This can lead to career advancement as you demonstrate an ability to add tangible value to the organization. For entrepreneurs, the role is vital. It is the necessary mindset to balance risk, understand market trends, and wisely manage resources.

In your personal life: On a personal level, the Investor Role can help you achieve better financial stability and security. You seek to make sound, or at least better, financial decisions, such as budgeting, saving for retirement, investing in a home or business, and planning for future expenses. When you focus on clearly understanding our financial standing and your personal goals, you can take steps that lead to a more stable and financially secure life. It can also enhance your intellectual growth as it requires continuous learning in the arenas of financial management, strategic planning, and resource acquisition and allocation.

In summary, embracing the Investor Role can foster financial security, professional growth, and robust social networks. It's a vital role to play as it ensures a focus on goals that are worth seeking.

"Someone is sitting in the shade today because someone planted a tree a long time ago." — *Warren Buffett*

IF YOU PLAY THE INVESTOR ROLE

The Investor Role requires a focus on value while practicing patience and diplomacy. It's worth the effort. Here is what this role can offer you.

Stability Strategist: You value and target financial stability. By managing your resources effectively, you can influence long-term financial success for yourself and those you care about, providing peace of mind.

Resource Expert: You have confidence in handling resources, like money, time, and people. This can lead to increased self-confidence and a feeling of control over your own life.

Opportunity Analyst: By analyzing opportunities and risks, you'll develop enhanced decision-making abilities that extend beyond finances.

Deal Diplomat: You learn to negotiate deals effectively, a skill that can be useful in many of life's situations.

Patient Planner: This role is patient, willing to invest in longer term strategies which applies to all arenas of life, both personal and professional.

Resource Multiplier: With your excellent resource management, you have the potential to make a positive impact on your world.

Cause Champion: You can contribute to causes you care about, driving change and influencing outcomes.

Shareholder Networker: You'll actively build a broad network of valuable connections. The emphasis here is on 'valuable'. Thoughtfully chosen, trustable contacts are the goal.

Financial Scholar: As you play the Investor Role, you'll learn more about money management, investments, and financial planning.

Thorough Decision Maker: This role knows that success takes time. Playing this role will teach you the virtue of waiting for investments of all kinds to yield returns, a mindset that is helpful in life in general. No more impulsive decisions.

Let's return to the example story with Fiona. What would her life look like if she began to apply this role?

Story Part 2: Fiona

[Fiona: one year later.] Fiona learns about the Investor Role during a local business owners' meeting, where a successful entrepreneur talks about the importance of playing different roles in a business. As she listens, she realizes she's been neglecting the Investor Role in her bakery. This revelation is a wake-up call. She starts researching and educating herself about financial management, and immediately begins applying the Investor Role principles to her business.

She starts by assessing her bakery's current profitability. It's a daunting task, but she's determined. She discovers that some of her most popular pastries aren't making enough profit due to the high cost of ingredients. She also learns that her bakery has been bleeding money due to inefficient use of resources. This knowledge is hard to swallow, but it also gives her a clear direction.

Next, Fiona begins to negotiate with her suppliers. It's unfamiliar and challenging, but she persists. Over time, she secures better deals, bringing down the cost of her ingredients without compromising on quality.

She then focuses on building a strategic professional network. She attends local business events, forms alliances with other entrepre-

neurs, and becomes more selective about who she associates with professionally. Her network begins to evolve from a stagnant pond to a dynamic, flowing river, bringing in new opportunities and valuable business connections.

In addition, she starts communicating better with her employees about the bakery's financial health. She considers ways to extend profits to her employees based on new growth. After consulting with others to gather the necessary information needed to make this decision, she shares a profit sharing strategy with her employees. This brings a new sense of camaraderie and purpose to the team. They work together with a collective focus on making the business a success.

Finally, Fiona begins budgeting and tracking the bakery's expenses diligently. It's still not her favorite part of the business, but she begins to see it as a necessary tool to ensure her bakery's sustainability. She even finds that now that her finances are not a chaotic mess, she no longer avoids them. Addressing her financial matters begins to feel more like a task on a to-do list than a suffocating tidal wave of pressure.

Over time, Fiona's bakery begins to show measurable improvement. It's not an overnight success—the Investor Role requires patience and long-term vision—but she starts seeing a steady increase in her profits.

More importantly, she feels more in control of her business's destiny and has a clearer understanding of how to guide it towards success. The charm of the bakery remains, but now it's complemented by a strong financial foundation.

"If you don't understand something, you need to surround yourself with people who are smarter than you, and move forward with your vision." -Kathy Ireland

---

THE INVESTOR ROLE BULLETED

The best investment is the one with the results that you value.

Financially Savvy: Possesses deep understanding of financial principles and markets. Exudes curiosity about market trends and investment opportunities. Does not avoid money issues or money talk. Understands financial principles and how to apply them.

Profit-Focused: Displays a keen attention to the bottom line. Can recognize value in investments, including people, projects, and opportunities. Consistently aims for growth.

Skillful Negotiating Skills: Engages in discussions to reach mutually beneficial agreements. Able to secure beneficial agreements while maintaining relationship.

Relationship-Valuer: Values relationships and understands their impact on profitability and successful outcomes. Manifests integrity and transparency in dealings.

Sustainability: Prioritizes long-term viability over short-term gains. Values efficient use of resources like time and money.

Patient: Exhibits patience. Understands that significant returns often require time. Maintains course in volatile situations.

Talent-Spotter: Has a knack for identifying talent and resources necessary for results. Actively seeks and nurtures beneficial relationships.

Budget-Designer: Designs and maintains an effective budget and regularly assesses financial health while identifying areas for improvement. Looks for cost-trimming opportunities.

Proactive approach: Takes action to secure resources and opportunities, rather than waiting for them to come along.

Generous: Displays both personal and professional generosity.

If this role is unused or underdeveloped:

- Financial instability.
- Unhealthy relationship with money and/or other resources.
- Missed opportunities.

If this role is overused:

- Overly frugal.
- Creates dependency.
- Transactional mindset in relationships.

*"The stock market is filled with individuals who know the price of everything,
but the value of nothing." -Philip Fisher*

THE INVESTOR ROLE DESCRIBED

Embracing the Investor Role is about being open to learning, practicing, and applying strategic thinking to maximize riches. But riches aren't just about money—they include time, relationships, opportunities, knowledge, and every resource that holds value.

People often assume this role is about money, but in reality, it's about **value**—recognizing it, growing it, and using it wisely. When you adopt this role, you leave behind any fear or insecurity about "money" and move into a mindset of curiosity, seeking ways to develop your personal and professional financial strategy.

This role focuses on more than just monetary gain. It involves finding, recognizing, and maximizing value in everything you invest in—whether people, projects, opportunities, or time. The Investor Role thrives on maximizing all available resources to create success.

And the best investments aren't always financial. Playing the Investor Role well means applying the same level of strategic foresight to career decisions, personal growth, and relationships as one would to financial assets. It's about weighing risks against rewards, maximizing opportunities, and making deliberate choices that lead to long-term success.

Investors are skilled at allocating resources efficiently. Whether it's money, talent, time, or connections, they understand that strategic investments—made with discipline and foresight—yield greater returns in the long run. They make the most of what they have, using it as a foundation for greater growth.

Investors recognize potential in people, projects, and ideas. Like Luminaries, they inspire others, but instead of rallying crowds, they build and sustain personal and trustworthy partnerships. They don't

APPRECIATING THE INVESTOR ROLE

just collect contacts—they cultivate meaningful connections that drive lasting success.

And while this role does maintain an attentive focus on the bottom line, it does so while continuously investing in stronger partnerships. Those who master the Investor Role understand the lasting impact of relationships on success. Their ability to see value where others might not allows them to identify opportunities others might overlook.

Those in this role negotiate with integrity, balancing ambition with fairness. They seek win-win scenarios, knowing that the best deals foster lasting success for all.

The Investor Role focuses on the strategic steps that lead to financial success. But this isn't a get-rich-quick mindset. Instead, it's learning to recognize long-term potential and to pursue it with discipline. Investors are patient, understanding that significant returns often require time.

Sustainability is central to the Investor Role. Long-term rewards outweigh short-term gains, and every resource—time, money, or energy—is used with lasting impact in mind. Wise Investors think beyond the present, ensuring their choices create stability and opportunity for future generations.

The Investor Role embraces budgeting, viewing it not as a restriction but as a strategy for growth. They constantly assess financial health, refine spending, and seek efficiencies. Embracing the wisdom that *"a penny saved is a penny earned,"* they take pride in managing resources with precision, ensuring wealth—of any kind—is both sustained and multiplied.

This is why generosity is a defining feature of the Investor Role when played well. Those who master it understand that true wealth—whether financial, relational, or personal—is meant to be shared. They invest in people, communities, and causes, knowing that real success isn't just about accumulation, but about contribution.

"To whom much is given, much is expected," is an appropriate adage for the Investor Role. The best Investors don't just seek gains; they seek to build, sustain, and give back. They recognize that wealth—of any kind—isn't just a personal asset, but a tool for greater good.

"To give away money is an easy matter and in any man's power. But to decide to whom to give it, and how large, and when, and for what purpose and how, is neither in every man's power nor an easy matter."
-Aristotle

INVESTOR ROLE PRACTICED

This section offers practical activities with examples to help you practice the Investor Role. The journey to embody this role involves three steps, starting with the most crucial and possibly the most difficult: adopting the Investor mindset.

A mindset is the foundation upon which our decisions, behaviors, and interactions are built. To step into the Investor Role, you need to adopt the mindset that will guide your actions in this new direction. The most important trait is also the most challenging for those who rarely play this role and that is to not fear or avoid thinking about financial matters. Begin with that as you read the mindset traits that will help you develop this role.

Step 1: Adopt the Mindset of the Investor Role

Financially Savvy: You possess an enthusiastic and growing understanding of financial matters.

Profit-Focused: You have a sharp focus on the bottom line. Budgeting is a positive activity.

Relationship-Valuer: You prioritize the time and investment it takes to develop worthwhile relationships.

Patient: You understand that significant returns often require time and you are not easily knocked off this course.

Proactive: You are future-oriented, not waiting for resources and opportunities to come to you but actively seeking them out. You think long-term.

Thinking like the Investor Role is a big first step in using this role well. A worthwhile investigation before you move on to Step 2 would be to assess each of the above over the course of a week. How often do you think like the Investor Role? That will give you helpful clues into which activities might be most beneficial.

Step 2: Choose an Activity to Practice the Role

The next section contains a range of activities designed to help you think like and practice the Investor Role. All the activities align with the characteristics of the Investor and when practiced will help you refine and ultimately internalize this role. For many, this role is one of the most challenging because of the negatives that might be attached to thinking about "money." Try to view this role as much more than being "money" focused. It's more about being focused on value. The Investor frequently asks themselves "Is this worth it?".

Step 3: Repeat

Practicing these activities consistently will enable these new mindset traits to become second nature. The more you practice, the more adept you will become at embodying the Investor Role. Remember, transformation doesn't happen overnight. Be patient investing in yourself.

"The greatest wealth is to live content with little." -Plato

PRACTICAL EXERCISES: INVESTOR

This is the practice section for the Investor Role. If you want to build up this role, read through this section and choose activities that will challenge you. All the roles can be improved no matter how well or how poorly you play a role. But don't try all these exercises at once. It would be overwhelming and not what the Investor Role would do. Invest your time toward the activities that will offer you the greatest return. Think: What activity would bring me the most value? You are choosing your activity like the Investor Role would.

Create a Budget: Develop a personal or business budget, identifying income, necessary expenses, and potential areas for cost reduction. Update and review it regularly to track your financial health and make informed decisions.

Ellen, a mom of two, found herself living paycheck to paycheck, unsure of where her money was going each month. To regain control of her finances, she began by tracking all her expenses and income. She created a budget, allocating specific amounts for necessities like rent, utilities, groceries, and childcare. She also set aside a small portion for savings. Over time, Ellen was able to reduce her debt, start saving, and even begin to save for a vacation with her kids.

Follow the Market: Start following financial news, stock market trends, or industry-specific financial reports. Aim to understand the dynamics and principles driving these trends.

Samuel, a recent college graduate, received a investment gift from his grandfather—a small amount of stock. Determined to honor his grandfather's gift, Samuel began reading financial news, researching companies, and following market trends.

As he delved deeper, Samuel found himself captivated by the intricacies of the stock market. He learned to analyze various factors that influence stock prices and developed a keen eye for spotting investment opportunities. Gradually, he gained confidence in making more informed decisions.

This initial spark ignited a newfound passion for investing in Samuel's life. Over time, he began applying his knowledge not only to the stocks gifted by his grandfather but also to other investment opportunities. His journey transformed an initial gift into a valuable skill set.

Investment Simulation: Participate in an online stock market simulation game. This will allow you to experience investment decision-making without risking real money.

Susan, a high school teacher, wanted to introduce her students to the world of finance. She found an online stock market simulation game and incorporated it into her economics class. Through the game, students were able to make investment decisions, see the outcome of these decisions, and adjust their strategies. The students gained a hands-on understanding of the stock market and investing.

Networking: Make a conscious effort to expand your professional network. Attend industry events or join online forums. Aim to connect with individuals who can provide valuable insights, partnerships, or opportunities.

Jeremy works in commercial real estate and understands the importance of expanding his professional network. He makes a conscious effort to attend industry events and join relevant forums, consistently seeking to connect with individuals who can provide valuable insights or opportunities.

Through his proactive approach, Jeremy has met key figures in the real estate market, including developers, investors, and other professionals. One connection in particular stood out—an investor with whom Jeremy built a strong relationship. This partnership eventually led to a major real estate deal, opening doors to new projects and opportunities.

Inspire Collaboration: Encourage everyone's input and work towards a consensus on an issue or project. Make sure everyone's ideas and opinions are appreciated.

When planning a family vacation, Anne took an Investor's approach— seeing it as an investment in shared experiences and lasting memories. Rather than choosing a destination on her own, she gathered input from each family member, balancing individual interests with a collective vision.

Through thoughtful negotiation, she ensured everyone had something to look forward to. She researched deals, planned activities strategically, and optimized the schedule for both fun and relaxation. By thinking ahead and facilitating win-win solutions, Anne created a trip that wasn't just enjoyable—it strengthened family bonds and made everyone feel valued.

Negotiation Skills: Practice negotiation in day-to-day situations. It could be negotiating a better price for a product or service, or negotiating terms in a business deal.

Carmen, a small business owner, usually avoided negotiating with suppliers for her store. She found it intimidating and often accepted prices as they were—until she realized how much she was leaving on the table.

Determined to improve, she started by reading books on negotiation and practicing in small, everyday situations. Gradually, she applied her skills to business deals, gaining confidence with each conversation. Over time, Carmen secured better terms with her suppliers, saving money and strengthening her business.

Mentorship: Seek out a mentor in the field of investment or business. Learning from someone experienced can be highly beneficial.

Jasmine, a young professional interested in investing, realized that her knowledge and experience in this field were too limited. She decided to seek out a mentor and eventually connected with Irina who she met at a local women's business meetup. Irina worked in the investment industry and had decades of experience in investing. She was at a point in her life where giving back was a priority for her so she was happy to offer input and suggestions for Jasmine.

Over the next year, Irina imparted valuable knowledge and practical tips to Jasmine, from deciphering market trends to making informed investment decisions. Jasmine's confidence and ability in investing grew significantly, and she attributed much of her progress to the mentorship she received from Irina.

Investment Analysis: Pick a company and analyze its financial health, potential for growth, and investment viability. Go deep on this one. Learn everything you can about the company and how it *works*. Become an expert in this chosen company.

Oliver, a software engineer, had always focused on the technical aspects of his work. But as he gained experience, he became curious about how financial decisions shaped the company's future. Wanting to expand his perspective, he decided to analyze his own company's financial health, looking beyond code and product development.

He studied financial reports, profit margins, and cost structures, gaining insight into how engineering decisions impacted the bottom line. He also researched market trends, competitive positioning, and investment viability, learning how financial strategy influenced long-term growth.

Through this process, Oliver developed a new skill set—one that not only helped him think like the Investor Role but also improved his decision-making as an engineer. Now, when evaluating new projects, he considers not just technical feasibility but also business impact, making him a more strategic and valuable contributor to his company.

Resource Allocation: Engage in an activity that requires careful allocation of limited resources. It could be a project at work, planning a trip within a budget, or even a game that requires strategic use of resources.

As the farm manager, Leo is constantly optimizing resources, always thinking ahead to ensure the country farm runs efficiently. From managing the feeding schedules of cows and chickens to protecting the farm from predators, Leo focuses on maximizing every resource available.

For example, instead of simply upgrading the feeding system, Leo adjusted feeding times and reduced waste, improving both productivity and cost-efficiency. He also implemented a rotation system for grazing, allowing the land to recover while increasing its output.

By consistently fine-tuning operations and working with suppliers to secure the best deals, Leo ensures the farm operates at its best through his commitment to making the most of every asset.

Generosity Practice: Make a conscious effort to be strategically generous. It could be donating to a cause you care about, mentoring someone by investing your time, or sharing your skills and knowledge within your network of connections.

Fleet, a successful entrepreneur, decided to make generosity a more conscious part of his life. He started by making a significant donation to a local charity that supports underprivileged youth, something he had a personal connection to. He also set up a mentorship program for young entrepreneurs in his community, offering to share his business knowledge and experience.

This practice of generosity not only benefited others but also enriched Fleet's life and gave him a broader perspective on the power and the ultimate purpose of his resources.

Learn from Mistakes: Reflect on past financial decisions that did not turn out well. Identify what went wrong and what you could have done differently. This process of reflection promotes learning if the focus is on changing and not regret.

Cora was an enthusiastic beginner investor. However, a few years ago, she made a substantial investment in a company that ended up failing, resulting in a significant financial loss.

Rather than letting this experience deter her, Cora decided to learn from her mistake. She spent time analyzing what went wrong and realized she had failed to properly assess the risks involved. In her enthusiasm to invest, she stretched too far and used resources she could not afford to lose.

This experience was a wake-up call for Cora, making her a more cautious and better informed investor. From then on, she made sure to carry out comprehensive risk assessments before making investment decisions.

When you feel like you have a grasp on this role and the mindset and behaviors that motivate it, move on to the next section where you take its role play up to next level.

"Opportunities multiply as they are seized." — Sun Tzu

ADVANCED TIPS FOR PLAYING THE INVESTOR ROLE

Mastering the Investor Role requires…an investment. While this is true of all Seven Roles, people tend to be either all in or all out with this one. The Investor Role is one of the most polarizing roles, often appearing as a top strength for some and nearly absent for others.

If you're just beginning to develop this role, it may take extra patience and intentional effort to reach a level of comfort. The same principle that defines great investors—long-term strategic thinking—applies to growing this role. Playing the Investor Role is an investment in your future, requiring steady learning, small calculated steps, and patience—growth takes time.

If this is already one of your strongest roles, you may be well aware of its advantages but less aware of its potential pitfalls. Avoiding these drawbacks is a worthy undertaking, even when—and perhaps especially when—you play this role well or often.

Let's explore strategies from both perspectives—those who underplay this role and those who overplay it.

I Rarely Play This Role!

If this role doesn't come naturally, your goal isn't to jump in all at once—that's a risky approach, and ironically, a well-played Investor Role is all about making calculated, measured, and strategic moves. Instead, you'll want to develop this role in stages, much like an actual investor builds a diversified portfolio.

Step 1: Track and Measure What You Already Have

You can't invest wisely if you don't know what you have to work with. Start by auditing your financial habits, time usage, and relationships. This really is the first step to begin to practice this role and it will likely be even harder than you already think it will be. Think: small steps!

• Track Your Spending – Before making any investment decisions, spend two weeks tracking every dollar you spend. Where is your money actually going?

• Audit Your Time – Keep a log of where your time goes. How do you invest your time?

• Assess Your Relationships – Identify which relationships bring value to your life and which ones don't.

This step isn't about changing anything yet—just building awareness, like an investor studying the market before making a move.

Step 2: Build a Low-Risk Investment Habit

Once you understand your resources, the next step is to begin investing—but very slowly and with small, controlled amounts.

• Financially: Set aside $10 a week into a savings or investment account—purely as an exercise in discipline. This is about habit-building, not wealth accumulation.

• Time Management: Dedicate 30 minutes a week to something that grows your skills or long-term success (reading, professional development, networking). Or, commit to a structured daily schedule, even if only for part of the day.

• Relationship Investment: Once a week, reach out to someone whose relationship with you is worth strengthening—mentor someone, reconnect with a valuable contact, or express gratitude to a supporter.

The goal is to begin shifting into the Investor mindset—thinking long-term and making intentional choices. Small, consistent changes outperform large, impulsive ones.

Step 3: Practice Opportunity Evaluation

A core Investor skill is the ability to weigh risk vs. reward before committing to something. Use these exercises to develop that mindset:

• Before making any purchase over $50, pause and ask:

  • Will this add long-term value to my life?
  • Will I still appreciate it a year from now?
  • Is there a better place to invest this money?

• Before committing to a new project or time investment, ask:

  • Will this lead to personal or professional growth?
  • What is the likely return on this time investment?
  • Am I doing this out of obligation, or does it align with my long-term goals?

Risk is an inherent part of the investment process—whether financial, time-related, or relational. As you gain experience, you'll develop an intuition for understanding which risks are worth taking. But while you're still learning, take very small steps.

> **Warning:** If your goal with the Investor Role is financial, practice with simulations, **not real money**. Don't invest what you cannot afford to lose. Start by saving, not spending.

FRUGALITY IS ONE OF THE TRUEST AND MOST IDENTIFIABLE HALLMARKS OF THIS ROLE.

Slow and Steady

Developing the Investor Role is a process, not an overnight shift. By taking small, intentional steps—tracking resources, making low-risk investments, and evaluating opportunities—you'll gradually build confidence in this role. Over time, these habits will compound, strengthening your ability to make strategic decisions that lead to long-term success.

APPRECIATING THE INVESTOR ROLE

But just as underplaying this role has its challenges, overplaying it comes with its own set of risks. Let's explore what happens when the Investor Role is taken too far or used too much.

"Do what you can, with what you have, where you are." — Theodore Roosevelt

---

OverPlaying Investor Role

Those who play this role well are highly focused on value, outcomes, and profitability. This can be a tremendous strength, but it can also make the Investor Role appear—or even become—**too focused on results.**

In the classic short story *Silas Marner* by George Eliot, the main character begins as a man with meaningful relationships, but over time, he loses his regard for people and finds his purpose solely in the pursuit of money. His life becomes isolated, transactional, and empty, consumed by accumulating wealth rather than experiencing life. If you want to understand the wrong approach to the Investor Role, his story is a powerful cautionary tale.

This attitude is often what people fear when they resist learning to play the Investor Role. And for those who naturally embrace it, this is the impression they often have to defend against—the idea that they are purely in pursuit of gain as the ultimate goal.

Here are four strategies to avoid that pitfall while keeping the Investor Role a force for positive impact.

- Don't Ignore the Humans
- Helping Without Enabling

- Beware of Excessive Frugality
- When Money Takes Over Meaning

Let's start with the first one which is a reminder to retain a people focus.

1. Don't Ignore the Humans

As you grow in the Investor Role, you may become highly skilled in analyzing data, assessing risks, and spotting opportunities. However, if you rely too heavily on logic and efficiency, you risk reducing relationships to transactions rather than meaningful connections. Over time, this mindset can make others feel undervalued, leading to strained relationships both personally and professionally. A business leader, for example, may prioritize profit margins over employee well-being, only to find that low morale and high turnover ultimately hurt long-term success.

It can also play out in personal relationships. Someone focused on maximizing efficiency might begin viewing time spent with family as something to be optimized rather than enjoyed. A parent, for instance, might constantly calculate the "productive use" of family activities, measuring them against work commitments. If an evening with their children doesn't seem to produce a tangible return—like teaching a skill or reinforcing a lesson—they may feel like it's a waste rather than a valuable investment in connection. Over time, this perspective can erode relationships, making loved ones feel like they have to "prove" their worth rather than simply being valued.

To play this role well, you need to consider the value of your interactions—whether with people, time, or money. But this is also where the challenge lies. The very mindset that makes the Investor Role powerful can, if unchecked, lead to transactional thinking, strained relationships, or an overemphasis on returns.

As you practice this role, keep these simple guidelines in mind—to help prevent losing your compassion along the way:

- Make people-first decisions – Ask yourself: How does this investment impact others? Does it help them grow, or just serve my interests?
- Invest in non-monetary value – Focus on mentorship and community impact, not just financial gains.
- Balance logic with intuition – Data matters, but so do trust, relationships, and vision. Not everything worth investing in can be measured.
- Learn when to set aside the Investor mindset – Not every moment in life needs to be optimized; some are meant to be simply lived and enjoyed.

Remember: Wealth isn't just about what you gain, but what you give – The best Investors create lasting value not just for themselves, but for others.

2. Helping Without Enabling

One of the greatest strengths of the Investor Role is the ability to help others succeed. A well-played Investor Role lifts others up by providing resources, opportunities, and guidance. But when overplayed, this strength can shift from empowerment to enabling—creating dependence rather than growth.

Providing excessive financial or time resources without accountability can lead to unintended consequences. Constantly bailing out struggling businesses, friends, or family members may offer short-term relief but can ultimately prevent them from developing the skills needed for long-term success.

When an Investor takes too much responsibility for someone else's progress—especially when that person is not putting in effort—it creates an imbalance. Instead of fostering growth, it can reinforce reliance, making it harder for the individual to become self-sufficient.

Here are some ways to ensure your support strengthens rather than weakens:

Support with structure – Offer help in a way that builds confidence and capability. Encouraging independence ensures your investment has a lasting impact.

Know when to step back – Not every investment leads to success, and that's okay. If someone isn't taking ownership of their growth, trust that stepping back may allow them to rise on their own.

Set healthy boundaries – Your role is to invest wisely, not to carry the full burden. Focus your time and energy on those who are ready to put in the effort.

Teach, don't just give – Knowledge is the most valuable investment. When you provide guidance alongside resources, you help others develop the skills to sustain success on their own.

A well-balanced Investor Role creates opportunities, builds confidence, and fosters long-term success—not just for you, but for those you choose to invest in.

3. Beware of Excessive Frugality

The greatest strengths of the Investor Role can also be its greatest challenges—especially when it comes to frugality. At its best, this role is about wisely managing resources, ensuring every investment serves a purpose. But when overplayed, frugality can turn into miserliness, where relentless cost-cutting and financial return take priority over joy, satisfaction, or even basic needs.

This can manifest in subtle and not-so-subtle ways—skipping vacations or family events because they don't offer a tangible return, over-analyzing every expense to the point where daily life becomes a balance sheet, or sacrificing generosity and spontaneity in favor of rigid financial discipline. A well-played Investor Role balances financial wisdom with a life well-lived.

Here are some way to keep your focus on both saving—and spending.

- Set a "spend with purpose" rule – Allocate money, time, and energy toward experiences that bring joy and strengthen relationships, not just financial growth.
- Recognize non-financial returns – Some investments, like family time, hobbies, or community engagement, yield rewards that money never can.

Wealth is most meaningful when used well. Accumulating without enjoying misses the whole point of mastering this role.

4. When Money Takes Over Meaning

The Investor Role, at its core, is about maximizing value—and in many cases, that means financial value. Those who play this role well understand money's power: it creates opportunity, security, and influence. But when money becomes the only metric of success, the Investor Role can spiral into obsession. Wealth turns into a scoreboard, and every decision is weighed solely on profit potential, often at the cost of well-being, relationships, and personal fulfillment.

An unchecked focus on financial growth can lead to stress, tunnel vision, and a transactional view of life. Some Investors find themselves checking market trends compulsively, chasing the next big opportunity, or hesitating to spend money—even when it would bring joy or meaningful experiences. Family vacations, hobbies, and even basic comforts can feel like unnecessary expenses rather than worthwhile investments in a well-rounded life. In extreme cases, relationships suffer because personal interactions are evaluated in terms of financial worth rather than genuine connection.

Here are some things to think about as you think about money.

- Define what wealth actually means to you – Is your financial success tied to security, freedom, generosity, or something else? Clarify your end goal so money serves your vision rather than consuming it.

- Invest in life, not just in assets – Set a budget for enjoyment. Prioritize experiences, personal development, and giving, just as you would financial investments.
- Don't let numbers dictate emotions – Markets fluctuate. Opportunities come and go. Managing emotions is key.

Money is a powerful tool, but it's just that—a tool. The best Investors don't just accumulate wealth; they know when and how to use it.

Summarizing Advanced Tips

Playing the Investor Role well is about more than just making smart decisions—it's about mastering the balance between strategy and sustainability, generosity and discipline, long-term planning and present fulfillment.

For those who underplay this role, the key is to start small. Learning to track resources, take calculated risks, and invest wisely—whether in finances, relationships, or personal growth—builds confidence over time. The Investor Role isn't about immediate wins; it's about long-term vision. Developing patience, consistency, and a mindset that values strategic decision-making will transform how you approach wealth in all its forms.

For those who overplay this role, the challenge is different: remembering that wealth—financial and otherwise—is meant to be used well. Maximizing return on investment is important, but when money, efficiency, and optimization become the only measures of success, life loses its richness. The best Investors know when to step back, enjoy what they've built, and invest in things that have no monetary return—like family, joy, and community.

Ultimately, the Investor Role isn't just about accumulation—it's about building something greater. Whether it's a financial legacy, a thriving career, or meaningful relationships, this role is most powerful when used with wisdom, balance, and generosity.

"We make a living by what we get, but we make a life by what we give." — Winston Churchill

It's Worth It

In the theater of life, one role stands clear,
The Investor, wise, drawing resources near.
With deep insight into cost and gain,
Seeking opportunities like drops of rain.

They negotiate with tact, securing the deal,
Relationships treasured, their appeal.
Spotting talent, resources in their sight,
Budgeting with care, finances just right.

Yet beyond wealth, their vision spans,
Touching lives, extending hands.
Generosity their trademark, kind their word,
Their impact on hearts is truly heard.

Fostering growth and sharing abound,
The Investor Role influence is world renowned.
A balance of gaining and giving they find,
The Investor Role, a mastermind.

With wisdom and foresight, they quietly steer,
Investing in futures year after year.
Not just in profit, but people and place—
The Investor Role leaves a lasting trace.

SUMMARY

The Investor Role focusses on value, strategy, and sustainability—not just in finances, but in all resources, including time, relationships, and opportunities. At its core, this role is a multiplier—investing wisely to create growth and impact. Whether in business, personal development, or community contributions, mastering this role means striking a balance between acquisition and generosity, ensuring that success is not just a personal gain but shared with others.

Everyone needs to play this role—because this is the role that supplies generosity. And you cannot give what you do not have. Learning to manage resources effectively allows you to build a future where both you and those around you thrive.

This chapter provided strategies to strengthen your Investor Role, whether you are just beginning or already play it well. Developing this role is one of the smartest investments you can make.

Invest well. But, even more importantly, **invest wisely**.

"Generosity is the investment that never fails." -Henry David Thoreau

---

ONE QUICK TIP

This role is not about getting a bigger paycheck. This role is about everything that leads to a bigger paycheck.

A simple yet incredibly powerful tip is to keep a financial journal. This doesn't have to be complicated or time-consuming. Just a few minutes each day to jot down your expenses, savings, investments, and even thoughts about money and resources can be incredibly beneficial.

Reflect on your spending patterns, savings goals, and your overall attitude towards money. Are there any habits you'd like to change? Do you have a clear understanding of where your money goes? This practice helps you develop an understanding of financial principles in a personal, practical way. Over time, you'll become more mindful about your resources. It can also help you feel more comfortable, and less fearful, around money issues.

Remember, as with any role, the Investor Role is learned and developed over time. Start small, be consistent, and watch as your financial understanding and resource management skills grow.

ADVICE FROM AN INVESTOR

The beauty and power of the Investor Role is, to my mind, grossly underrated. This role is not just about money. It's about life. It's about relationships, about growth, and about understanding the world around us in ways that are far more profound and far-reaching than most people realize.

Many of us hear the word "investor" and immediately draw to mind images of Wall Street brokers, hedge fund managers, or wealthy tycoons making grandiose impersonal financial decisions. But I urge you to reconsider these preconceived notions. To be an investor doesn't require you to become a finance guru or to amass a fortune. It does ask you to be astute, patient, proactive, and generous. It requires a practiced understanding of seeing what is worth investing in and the critical ability to spot and nurture this value in the most unsuspecting of places.

In my own life, the Investor Role plays a principal role. It's helped me cultivate a forward-looking perspective, one that sees the potential in things and people before others do. It's made me understand that true wealth isn't made by hoarding resources, but rather by efficiently using what I have.

Perhaps most importantly, it's taught me to see the world around me in terms of opportunity, and to understand that my actions can help shape these opportunities for the better. Every decision I make, every interaction I have, is a chance to invest in a better future: for myself, for the people I care about, and for the world.

The world needs more people to take advantage of the Investor Role. It needs more individuals who see potential where others don't, who understand the importance of creating value, and especially more people willing to share that value with others.

So, I encourage you, whether you're an entrepreneur, a student, a homemaker, or a professional, use the Investor Role. Look for opportunities to invest in people, in ideas, and in your community. Learn to see potential where others see risk. Learn to be generous. The rewards you'll reap—both tangible and intangible—will be well worth the effort.

TRUSTING THE TEAM BUILDER ROLE
LIVING KINDLY

Are you empathetic in your interactions?
Do you value collaboration?
Are you supportive of and trusted by others?
Are you able to calm someone down?
This is the TEAM BUILDER ROLE!

WELCOME to the home of the Team Builder, where you feel comfortable, welcome and safe.

This is the role that harnesses the power of emotions and engages the gentler skills. At first glance, it might not seem as necessary as the other roles. It's not goal-driven, it doesn't rely on hard metrics, strategic roadmaps, or even immediate tangible results. But underestimate it at your peril—because this is the role that fuels ambition, sustains momentum, and ensures that everyone moves forward together.

The other six roles help you define and pursue your goals, but the Team Builder is what makes people genuinely care about the journey. It is the emotional glue that transforms a collection of individuals into a united, thriving team. More than a peacekeeper, the Team Builder Role develops a real trust which encourages collaboration, and ignites a shared passion that turns ideas into movements.

So, open your mind—and especially your heart—to this remarkable role. Unlike roles that measure success in tasks completed, the Team Builder measures it in relationships strengthened. It may not always seem like a traditional driver of success, but make no mistake—it is the force that galvanizes people, fosters harmony, and ultimately propels teams toward meaningful achievement.

Because at the end of the day, success isn't just about what we accomplish. It's about the connections of trust we build along the way. Prepare to feel.

"People will forget what you said, people will forget what you did, but people will never forget how you made them feel."— Maya Angelou

---

But what happens when those connections are neglected?

Let's meet Jea, a man who has mastered execution but struggles with the role that makes it all matter.

Story Part 1: Jea

[Jea: a 60 something "I am who I am" kind of person.] Jea is a highly accomplished project manager at a thriving tech company. With a sharp mind and relentless focus, he delivers results—on time, within budget, and with precision. His ability to foresee potential roadblocks and navigate complex technical challenges makes him invaluable. He excels in roles like the Prophet and Conceptualizer, guiding strategy and refining execution with ease.

But there's one role Jea doesn't play often—the Team Builder.

Jea believes that good results should be motivation enough, for himself and for his team. He sees emotional engagement as unnecessary fluff, something that slows progress rather than fuels it. When assigned team projects, he divides tasks methodically, expecting everyone to work independently. He avoids brainstorming sessions and sees group collaboration as inefficient.

In meetings, he's all business—no small talk, no casual check-ins. If someone raises a concern, he quickly dismisses it unless it directly impacts the bottom line. His no-nonsense demeanor is, at best, seen as endearing by a select few and, at worst, viewed as cold and detached.

His personal life mirrors his professional one. Jea keeps a small circle of acquaintances, but maintaining friendships is difficult. He struggles to invest in relationships or show emotional support, often viewing such efforts as distractions rather than necessities.

But recently, Jea has started to feel the consequences of his lack of the Team Builder Role. Despite his impressive track record, he's becoming increasingly isolated. His team's morale is slipping, productivity is declining, and turnover is rising. The best talent—those who value collaboration and connection—are choosing to work elsewhere.

Outside of work, the gaps are even harder to ignore. His inability to build and sustain meaningful relationships has left him feeling lonely, disconnected, and—though he would never admit it—unfulfilled.

For the first time, Jea is beginning to wonder: Is success enough if you have no one to share it with?

Despite his technical prowess and his professional success, the lack of genuine connection and expressed empathy is impacting his team's productivity and increasingly, his personal happiness.

We will see what adding the Team Builder role does for Jea but first let's look at how it might help you.

HOW CAN THE TEAM BUILDER ROLE HELP YOU?

The Team Builder Role is marked by its high emotional intelligence (EQ) with the ability to understand the nuances of both verbal and non-verbal communications. This role gets 'listening'.

In relationships: As a Team Builder, your empathy and high EQ allow you to tune into the emotional states of your loved ones, facilitating deeper, more meaningful connections. You bring a cooperative and supportive energy into your relationships, encouraging a nurturing environment in your home. Your ability to think in shades of grey promotes understanding and flexibility, enabling you to navigate complex personal dynamics openly.

Your perceptive nature encourages others to share their thoughts and feelings openly, leading to honest, trusting relationships. You are energized by personal projects that align with your values or contribute to a shared family vision, making your home a place of purpose and fulfillment.

In your career: In your professional life, the Team Builder Role enables you to build cohesive, high-performing teams. Your consensus-driven approach ensures all team members feel valued and heard, fostering a harmonious and productive work environment. Your natural ability to sense the mood of the group helps in conflict resolution and contributes to maintaining a positive work culture.

Your ability to understand relational complexities helps you navigate with relational agility. The trust you seem to naturally earn makes you a go-to person for advice or guidance. Your drive to work towards a purpose translates into passion, thereby leading to higher job satisfaction and performance.

In your personal life: In your social circles, your empathy, emotional intelligence, and your active listening skills make you a cherished friend and confidante. The ability to build consensus ensures every voice in your group is heard, reinforcing strong bonds of friendship. Your motivation to contribute to causes or visions resonates with others, often inspiring them to join you in social initiatives. The trust you cultivate in your social networks also allows for deeper, more rewarding and authentic interactions.

"What matters most in life are the connections you make with others."
—*Tom Ford*

The Team Builder role strengthens the ability to connect with others. Everyone can improve their ability to navigate emotions and thereby enhance relationships. It just takes practice and a willing heart.

IF YOU PLAY THE TEAM BUILDER ROLE

The Team Builder Role, when balanced effectively, can significantly enhance your personal, professional, and social life by fostering meaningful relationships, a fulfilling work environment, and offers the coveted prize: a purpose-driven life.

Relationship Builder: You have the capacity to build strong, deep relationships with an empathetic nature and high emotional intelligence.

Conflict Mediator: You can effectively mediate and resolve conflicts, as you understand different perspectives and value consensus over domination.

Emotional Tuner: You are attuned to the emotional states of those around you, enabling you to react appropriately and offer valued support.

Empathetic Listener: Your listening skills and encouraging nature foster an environment where others feel comfortable sharing their thoughts and feelings.

Cause Driven: You are motivated by tasks and projects that benefit a larger cause, which can lead to high personal and professional fulfillment.

Trust Cultivator: Your genuine interest in others and your willingness to collaborate rather than compete introduces real trust in personal, professional, and social settings.

Complexity Navigator: Your ability to think in terms of shades of grey rather than black and white helps you comprehend and navigate complex situations without judgement.

Team Supporter: Your cooperative and supportive nature can strengthen relationships and foster more collaborative environments.

Inclusivity Promoter: Your inclusive approach can lead to more cohesion at work and at home. People want to be on your team.

Mood Assessor: Your ability to accurately assess moods and emotions allows you to contribute positively to the environment, whether it's at home, at work, or in social settings.

Consummate Advocate – You stand up for others and champion their ideas, ensuring that every voice is heard and valued.

Story Part 2: Jea

[Jea: eight months later.] Jea knew something had to change. His team was struggling, and he could no longer ignore the signs—low morale, increased turnover, and stalled productivity. He had spent years believing that efficiency was about results, not relationships. But what if he had it backward?

At first, he approached the idea of developing his Team Builder Role as an experiment—something to test, rather than fully embrace. He started by reading about emotional intelligence and the role of empathy in leadership. He explored team-building strategies, selecting a few simple ideas to try.

His first shift was in meetings. Instead of rigidly sticking to the agenda, he opened space for his team to share concerns and opinions. To his surprise, this was well received. Encouraged, he introduced brainstorming sessions where the team could openly discuss current projects. In the very first session, a potential problem was identified early—something that, had it gone unnoticed, could have derailed the entire project. Seeing the value of collaboration in action, Jea immediately made these sessions a monthly practice.

Building on this momentum, Jea took another step—he worked on his listening skills. Instead of brushing past conversations, he focused on truly hearing what his team members had to say. He made an effort to understand their challenges, goals, and motivations.

At first, it felt forced and unnatural, but as his responses became more thoughtful, the shift in his team was undeniable. Productivity improved, engagement increased, and for the first time in years, turnover rates started to drop. His team wasn't just working harder— they were working together.

Inspired by these changes, Jea decided to extend his experiment beyond the office. He reached out to old friends and put more effort into new relationships. He listened more and spoke less. He showed interest in their lives—not out of obligation, but out of a growing understanding that connection mattered which turned into genuine interest.

The results were profound. His relationships, both personal and professional, started to thrive. He felt a sense of camaraderie and a sense of belonging he had never really felt before. As his projects at work became more successful, he realized that teamwork wasn't a distraction from productivity—it was the very thing that fueled it.

Jea's story underscores the fact that being technically competent isn't enough either for professional success or personal satisfaction. Genuine connection, empathy, and emotional intelligence—the hallmarks of the Team Builder

"A team is not a group of people who work together. A team is a group of people who trust each other." -Simon Sinek

THE TEAM BUILDER BULLETED

*Listening is more than a skill,
it's a demonstration of respect.*

Emotional Intelligence: Exhibits empathy and exercises high emotional intelligence to accurately assess moods or emotional states.

Relationship Management: Cooperative and supportive in relationships, promoting a sense of unity and mutual respect.

Consensus Building: Values collaborative decisions over dictatorial ones, fostering inclusiveness and shared responsibility.

Complex Thinking: Thinks in terms of shades of grey versus black and white, allowing for nuanced understanding and flexibility, without judgement.

Active Listener: Perceptive and listens well, encouraging others to express their thoughts and feelings.

Purpose Driven: Energized by tasks and projects that benefit a cause, a vision, or a purpose, offering others a sense of meaningful contribution.

Trust Builder: Gains trust easily. People feel comfortable sharing with the Team Builder Role as they feel genuine care and concern.

Emotional Support: Provides emotional support to others, attuned to others feelings.

Positivity Promoter: Uses their understanding of others' emotional states to nurture a positive and supportive environment.

Consummate Advocate: Champions others and ensures that every voice is heard, valued, and supported.

If this role is unused or underdeveloped:

- Unaware or unresponsive to emotional cues.
- Focused on self rather than on others.
- Slow to identify feelings and emotions in self and others.

If this role is overused:

- Emotional overload.
- People pleasing.
- Conflict avoidant.

THE TEAM BUILDER ROLE DESCRIBED

The Team Builder Role is essential for creating and maintaining strong, cohesive relationships in both personal and professional settings. Those who embody this role harness strong emotional intelligence— and respond to the needs of others. They are highly empathetic, able to feel what others feel, providing comfort and reassurance.

Team Builders are masters of relationship management. They are cooperative and supportive, constantly striving to foster relationships grounded in respect, trust, and mutual understanding. They recognize that each person brings unique skills and perspectives to the table and work to create an atmosphere where these contributions are valued and nurtured.

Consensus-building is at the heart of this role. Rather than dictating outcomes, Team Builders encourage collaboration and shared decision-making. They believe in the power of diverse perspectives and promote inclusivity, developing a sense of shared responsibility among team members. This consensus-driven approach helps ensure that everyone feels heard, validated, and invested in the team's success.

The Team Builder Role embraces shades of grey rather than rigid black-and-white thinking. They understand that situations are often complex, requiring a nuanced approach and the ability to see different perspectives. They value flexibility, adaptability, and the wisdom to compromise when necessary.

Possessing excellent listening skills, the Team Builder Role is perceptive and encouraging. They create an environment where others feel comfortable and safe expressing their thoughts, feelings, and ideas. They believe in the power of active listening as a tool for understanding and connection.

Team Builders are energized by tasks that align with a shared purpose. They understand that meaningful work extends beyond individual tasks and contributes to a larger vision. They motivate others to be a part of this bigger picture, part of a greater good.

Trust is a key aspect of the Team Builder Role. People feel at ease with those who play this role well, often sharing more than they might otherwise, due to the trust and rapport built. This ability to cultivate trust is crucial in fostering open and honest relationships within a team.

The Team Builder Role excels at providing emotional support, being attuned to the feelings and needs of others. They are a comforting presence in times of stress or challenge, offering reassurance and guidance. Their goal is to create a supportive and positive environment where everyone feels valued and understood.

At maximum play, the Team Builder Role is defined by a higher than average emotional intelligence, overt consensus-building, active listening, and trust-building. It intentionally creates an environment that is supportive, inclusive, and focused on a shared purpose. It develops and protects relationships so everyone can thrive. This role is crucial and its importance cannot be overstated.

"Be kind whenever possible. It is always possible."
-Dalai Lama

TEAM BUILDER ROLE PRACTICED

A mindset refers to a collection of attitudes and approaches that shapes how an individual perceives and interacts with the world. For the Team Builder Role, this draws more from the emotional side of communicating. And yes, it's learnable!

Step 1: Adopt the Mindset of the Team Builder Role

First, adopt the Team Builder mindset, characterized by empathy, collaboration, active listening, fostering inclusivity, and trust-building. This role relies heavily on emotional expertise.

Be Open and Non-Judgmental: Approach every interaction with an open mind and heart. Try not to make immediate judgments or assumptions about the person or the situation. Remember that everyone has their own story, their own experiences, and their own perspectives. It's crucial to respect these differences and seek to understand them, rather than to judge or dismiss them.

Prioritize Understanding: Focus on understanding the other person's thoughts, feelings, and perspectives. This means not just hearing the words they say, but also paying attention to their tone, body language, and emotional state. Seek to understand their experiences and feelings from their point of view.

Show Genuine Interest: Make an effort to be fully present and engaged during conversations. Show genuine interest in the person and what they are saying. This can be done through verbal cues like asking follow-up questions or non-verbal cues like maintaining eye contact and using responsive body language.

By adopting these attitudes and behaviors, one can better embody an empathetic, collaborative, and listening mindset. It's a journey that requires consistent effort and practice, but the rewards are worthwhile, as these traits can greatly enhance both personal and professional relationships.

Once you "put on" these mindset traits, you're ready to move onto the next step.

Step 2: Choose an Activity to Practice the Role

In the next section, with the mindset of a Team Builder, choose an activity to help you practice. This role requires tapping into your emotions, so keep that in mind as you seek to use it. You may find some of the activities uncomfortable as they ask you to be more emotive, even vulnerable, with others. Try them and start slowly. Practice with people you know, and maybe give them a heads up about what you are trying to learn.

Step 3: Repeat

Repeat and be patient. This requires time as most of the activities cannot be done quickly. By consistently practicing these activities, you'll be nurturing the Team Builder Role, which will help you create a more connected personal and professional environment.

PRACTICAL EXERCISES: TEAM BUILDER ROLE

This is the practice section for the Team Builder Role. If you want to build up this role, read through this section and choose activities that challenge you. As with most new behavior practices, the best and most effective one might be the one you want to do the least.

Emotional Intelligence Practice: Develop a daily habit of labeling your emotions throughout the day. This can help you become more attuned to your own feelings and, consequently, the feelings of others.

Alexander, *a project manager, felt overwhelmed with constant meetings and deadlines. Instead of ignoring these feelings, he started a simple journaling practice where he would jot down his emotions at different points during the day—when he woke up, during his lunch break, and before bedtime.*

Over time, Alexander began to understand his emotional patterns better, improving his ability to observe and manage his responses.

Relational Reflection Practice: Set aside time to reflect on your relationships—with coworkers, clients, friends, or family. What helped someone feel supported today? What could you have done differently?

Dr. Corene's strength as a Team Builder lies in her quiet commitment to relationships. Despite a full schedule, she sets aside time each evening to journal about her interactions—both at work and at home. Her journaling isn't just a habit; it's a relational tool.

After a long day, she reflects with questions like, "What helped today?" or "Where could I have been more present?" This daily practice helps her respond with more empathy and intention. She also writes about her family life, using the same lens of care and faith to guide how she shows up for those closest to her.

For Dr. Corene, journaling offers clarity, peace, and a deeper connection to the people in her life. By making reflection a regular practice, she strengthens both her awareness and her ability to support others with consistency and grace.

"To touch the soul of another human being is to walk on holy ground."
— Stephen R. Covey

Team Building Activities: Initiate a fun, engaging activity that requires cooperation from all participants.

Ariana, a department head at a fast-paced tech company, noticed her team struggling with collaboration and synergy. To address this, she organized an offsite retreat focused on team-building and creativity. Among the activities was a dynamic scavenger hunt that encouraged cooperation, problem-solving, and open communication.

As her team navigated the challenges, they tapped into each other's strengths, brainstorming solutions and celebrating small victories. The scavenger hunt fostered not only a sense of camaraderie but also sparked fresh ideas and perspectives. By the end of the retreat, Ariana saw a renewed spirit within the team, transforming their dynamics and enhancing their collaborative efforts back at the office.

Active Listening Practice: Focus on the speaker, resisting the urge to interrupt or plan your responses prematurely.

Michael often found himself listening to his teenage son, Elijah, only to critique or counter what he said. Instead of truly hearing Elijah's perspective, he focused on finding flaws or offering corrections. Over time, he realized this was creating distance between them.

Determined to change, Michael decided to practice active listening. Rather than preparing a response, he focused on being fully present, letting Elijah express his thoughts without interruption. He asked follow-up questions to understand, not to challenge.

This shift made a difference. Elijah felt heard and respected, which led to more open conversations. As a result, he became more interested in Michael's input, seeking his perspective rather than bracing for criticism.

By listening with the intent to understand rather than critique, Michael strengthened their relationship and fostered more meaningful discussions.

Conflict Resolution: Act as a mediator in a conflict, aiming for a solution that addresses the needs and concerns of those involved.

As a CEO, Robert manages multiple teams, ensuring that collaboration remains strong across the organization. When two department heads clashed over responsibilities on a critical project, their disagreement escalated, creating friction that threatened to derail progress. Each manager believed their team's priorities should take precedence, and neither was willing to compromise.

Robert stepped in—not to dictate a solution, but to facilitate a productive resolution. He met with each manager individually to understand their concerns, then brought them together to find common ground. Drawing on his expertise in conflict resolution, he reframed the issue from a competition over resources to a shared challenge that required cooperation. By guiding them toward a solution that valued both teams' contributions while keeping the project on track, he ensured a balanced and strategic outcome.

Over time, Robert's leadership set the standard for effective conflict management. His managers became more adept at resolving disputes on their own, strengthening interdepartmental collaboration and fostering a more cohesive, high-functioning organization.

Trust Building: Trust, from the perspective of the Team Builder Role, is measured by how much you care. Showing others that you value them as individuals with their own unique stories, experiences, and perspectives is a good first step.

James, a project manager, noticed that his team members were polite and professional with one another but didn't seem to have a deep level of trust. He decided to try a trust-building exercise during their next team meeting. He explained the rules of "Two Truths and a Lie." Each person would share three statements about themselves, two of which were true and one of which was a lie. The rest of the team would then try to guess which statement was the lie.

James went first to set the tone, sharing two true aspects of his personal life—his passion for hiking and his volunteer work at a local animal shelter—and one false statement about being an accomplished guitarist. His team members enjoyed guessing which statement was the lie, and it sparked a lively conversation about hiking, pets, and music.

As each team member took their turn, they learned more about each other's hobbies, families, and experiences. It broke down walls, helped them see each other as individuals beyond their professional roles, and laid the foundation for deeper trust. James noticed that, in the weeks following the exercise, his team communicated more freely and collaborated more effectively.

This small activity became a stepping stone towards fostering a more trusting, cohesive team environment.

Purpose-Driven Tasks: Engage in projects that resonate with your values and passions. The Team Builder Role follows their heart.

Jamie discovered a powerful healing modality that transformed her life, and she felt drawn to share it with others. Naturally skilled at connecting with people, Jamie wanted that for her clients—she envisioned a community where people could support each other on their healing journeys.

She started by organizing informal gatherings, encouraging each participant to contribute and connect with others who shared their interests. Jamie's approach was collaborative, focusing on empowering others.

As the community grew, Jamie celebrated their progress, hosted regular events, and fostered an online platform where members could connect. Her skill in the Team Builder Role transformed the group into a genuine support network, where healing became a shared journey, and each member felt valued.

Emotional Check-Ins: Regularly share and discuss feelings with your loved ones.

Lucy, a mother of two, initiated a daily dinner ritual where each family member would share something that made them happy and something that upset them that day. This practice not only improved family communication but also helped Lucy and her children better understand each other's emotional states.

Practicing Active Listening: Show genuine interest and empathy during conversations.

Ishy has a talent for making people feel truly heard, She focuses fully on the speaker, putting away distractions, maintaining eye contact, and nodding to show she's engaged. Instead of planning her response while others talk, she listens carefully, then asks thoughtful follow-up questions to encourage deeper conversation.

She also practices patience, resisting the urge to interrupt or immediately offer solutions. When a friend or colleague shares a concern, Ishy allows them to express themselves fully before responding. Her ability to listen with empathy reassures people that their thoughts matter, strengthening trust and connection.

By consistently practicing active listening, Ishy has built stronger relationships and made those around her feel valued. Her approach is a reminder that listening is a skill anyone can develop—with focus, patience, and genuine curiosity.

"When we listen with curiosity, we don't listen with the intent to reply. We listen for what's behind the words."
— Roy T. Bennett

Appreciating Different Perspectives: Make an effort to understand and respect diverse viewpoints.

During a heated debate about political policy, Noah and his friend found themselves on opposite sides of the issue. Rather than trying to "win" the argument, Noah focused on attentively listening and understanding his friend's perspective. He asked thoughtful questions, acknowledged valid points, and resisted the urge to interrupt or dismiss differing views.

Despite their disagreements, the conversation remained respectful and productive. Noah recognized that a good discussion doesn't require agreement—just a willingness to listen and engage with an open mind. In the end, their conversation not only preserved their friendship but also deepened Noah's understanding of the issue, proving that respectful dialogue can lead to growth on both sides.

Encourage Sharing: Cultivate an atmosphere that promotes open sharing of ideas and opinions.

As a book club coordinator, Lisa noticed that discussions were often dominated by a few outspoken members, while others remained silent. Recognizing the value of diverse perspectives, she made it a point to invite everyone into the conversation.

Rather than letting only the most vocal members steer the discussion, Lisa asked quieter participants for their thoughts, framed open-ended questions to encourage different viewpoints, and created a welcoming space where all opinions were valued.

By ensuring everyone had the opportunity to contribute, Lisa not only made each member feel heard but also enriched the discussion. The result was a more engaging, diverse conversation where members felt included, respected, and eager to participate.

Non-Verbal Practice: Practice recognizing the emotional states of others through non-verbal cues.

Dale, a therapist, knew that communication wasn't just about words—it was also about what wasn't being said. In his sessions, he noticed that clients often masked their true emotions, saying they were "fine" while their body language told a different story.

Determined to sharpen his ability to read non-verbal cues, Dale began focusing on the small but telling signs—a tightened jaw, shifting posture, averted eyes, or a hesitation before answering. Instead of relying solely on spoken words, he adjusted his approach based on what he observed.

One day, a teenage client insisted he wasn't upset, but Dale noticed his clenched fists and tense shoulders. Instead of pushing, Dale simply said, "It seems like something's weighing on you." That small acknowledgment opened the door for an honest conversation.

Over time, Dale's attention to non-verbal communication transformed his work. Clients felt more understood, families he worked with became more attuned to each other's emotions, and his ability to connect deepened. By listening with his eyes as well as his ears, Dale wasn't just hearing people—he was truly seeing them.

Learn How to Create a Safe Space: Facilitate an environment *where people feel comfortable expressing their emotions.*

Drake notices that Samuel has been unusually quiet in recent meetings. Instead of ignoring it or assuming it's not his place, he takes a moment after work to check in. With a calm and open demeanor, he asks, "Hey, I've noticed you've been quieter than usual. Is everything okay?"

Samuel hesitates at first but soon opens up, sharing that he's dealing with a difficult situation at home. Rather than rushing to offer advice or change the subject, Drake listens fully. He doesn't try to fix the problem—he simply makes room for Samuel to express himself without fear of judgment or dismissal.

By being present and allowing Samuel to be heard, Drake creates a conversation built on trust and respect. His ability to listen without pushing is a core strength of the Team Builder Role.

Learning to Say No: While it's important to actively support others in this role, it's equally important to maintain personal boundaries. Practice saying no when you're overcommitted or when something isn't aligned with your values. For instance, if a friend asks for a favor when you're already overwhelmed, politely explain your situation and suggest an alternative solution.

Emma, a compassionate friend, found herself facing this challenge. Her empathic nature made her an excellent listener and a shoulder to lean on. However, the downside was that people often turned to her with their problems. This was emotionally draining for Emma, and she found herself feeling overwhelmed by the emotional stories from others.

Recognizing this, Emma decided to practice saying "no" when she felt emotionally overextended. One evening, after a particularly stressful day at work, her friend Mia called, sounding upset and wanting to vent about a disagreement with her partner. Although Emma cared about Mia and wanted to support her, she also knew that she was emotionally exhausted and needed to prioritize her own mental wellbeing.

Gathering her courage, Emma said, "Mia, I really care about you and I want to be there for you. But I've had a tough day myself and I'm feeling quite drained. Can we talk tomorrow when I'm in a better place to support you? In the meantime, is there someone else you could talk to?" Mia understood and appreciated Emma's honesty, and they ended up having their conversation the next day when Emma felt more equipped to provide the emotional support Mia needed.

Learning to set boundaries in this way not only helped Emma maintain her emotional health, but also deepened her relationship with Mia by creating an environment of mutual respect and support.

Advocate for Others: Speak up when someone's strengths are overlooked.

Surya has worked with Daniel for several years and knows he is highly skilled, dedicated, and respected by the team. However, despite his strong performance, Daniel keeps getting passed over for promotions in favor of more outspoken colleagues. Surya notices that while Daniel doesn't always assert himself, his leadership qualities are evident in the way he approaches his work and the way others approach him.

During a leadership meeting, when management discusses candidates for an upcoming promotion, Surya speaks up:

> "Daniel has been instrumental in streamlining our processes and mentoring new team members. His contributions are a big part of why this department runs smoothly. I know he isn't the loudest voice in the room, but that's part of what makes him a great leader. He listens carefully, makes well-thought-out decisions, and brings out the best in others without needing to dominate the conversation. Those are exactly the qualities we need for this project."

His comment shifts the conversation, and management re-evaluates Daniel's contributions. By the next review cycle, Daniel is offered a well-earned promotion.

By advocating for Daniel and reframing his quiet approach as a collaborative leadership potential, he ensures others see the value.

"We rise by lifting others."— Robert Ingersoll

Empathy Practice: Consistently strive to understand others' feelings and perspectives. Put yourself in their position and imagine how you would feel.

Muriah, a physical therapist, works well with patients recovering from injuries and chronic pain. One patient, Esther, seemed especially *discouraged—missing appointments, withdrawing during sessions, and showing little motivation to continue her treatment.*

Instead of assuming Esther was unmotivated, Muriah put herself in her patient's shoes. She imagined what it would feel like to struggle with pain every day, to wonder if recovery was even possible. With that perspective in mind, she approached Esther with genuine curiosity and care. In a private conversation, she gently asked, "What has this experience been like for you?"

As Esther spoke, Muriah didn't just listen—she felt her frustration, her fear, her exhaustion. Rather than offering quick fixes, she acknowledged how difficult the journey must be. "That sounds incredibly tough. It makes sense that you'd feel this way."

That moment of true empathy changed everything. Esther no longer felt like just another patient going through the motions—she felt understood. Over the next few weeks, she became more engaged in her recovery, not because the treatment had changed, but because she knew someone truly cared.

Bringing It All Together

Building your Team Builder Role isn't about having all the answers or taking charge—it's about showing up for others in meaningful ways. Through active listening, trust-building, collaboration, or conflict resolution, these small but intentional actions can create stronger, more connected relationships—both personal and professional.

As you explore these exercises, challenge yourself to step outside your comfort zone. The most impactful growth often comes from the practices that feel the hardest at first. Pay attention to how your mindset shifts as you apply these skills, and notice how your ability to understand, support, and inspire others expands over time.

Every interaction is an opportunity to strengthen your role as a Team Builder—one conversation, one act of kindness, and one moment of connection at a time.

"Empathy has no script. There is no right or wrong way to do it. It's simply listening, holding space, withholding judgment, emotionally connecting, and communicating that incredibly healing message of 'You're not alone.'" -Brené Brown

ADVANCED TIPS FOR PLAYING THE TEAM BUILDER ROLE

The heart of the Team Builder Role is trust—a simple word, but a powerful one. Trust makes relationships stronger, communication easier, and collaboration feel safe. Whether at work or in life, trust changes everything. And building it is what the Team Builder Role is all about.

But trust can't be forced. It grows over time—through consistency, reliability, and a real understanding of others. That's where the Empathy Triad comes in: cognitive empathy (understanding), emotional empathy (feeling), and compassionate empathy (responding). Together, these form the foundation of real trust—and the core of the Team Builder Role.

To play this role well, you need to grow your empathy. To master it, you need to know how to protect it. We'll start with those who are learning to build empathy. Then we'll move on to those who already play this role well—and need to learn how to guard their emotional energy while still showing up for others.

Excelling in the Empathy Triad

If the Team Builder Role doesn't come naturally to you, don't worry. Empathy isn't something you either have or don't—it's something you can build. Like any skill, it grows with practice. Before we jump into how to strengthen it, let's take a moment to define what we mean by the Empathy Triad.

"No one cares how much you know, until they know how much you care." -Theodore Roosevelt

---

Types of Empathy

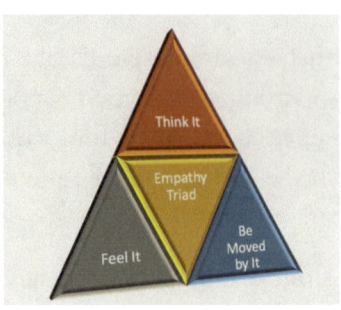

Empathy isn't just one thing—it's made up of three connected parts: **cognitive, emotional, and compassionate empathy**. Together, they form what we call the *Empathy Triad*. It's about understanding how someone else feels, actually *feeling* it with them, and then knowing when and how to respond with care. Let's look at each part more closely.

Cognitive Empathy – *Understanding what someone else is thinking*

This is the ability to mentally step into someone else's shoes. You might not feel what they're feeling, but you understand what's going on in their world. To strengthen it cognitive empathy try these:

- Active Listening – Give someone your full attention. No interrupting, no rushing to reply. Just listen to understand.
- Ask Open-Ended Questions – Instead of yes/no questions, try: *"What was that like for you?"*
- Reflect – After a conversation, take a moment to consider what you learned about their perspective.
- Seek Feedback – Ask, *"Did I get that right?"* or *"Is there more I should understand?"* It builds trust *and* skill.

Emotional Empathy – *Feeling what someone else is feeling*

This is when you truly connect with someone's emotions. Their joy feels contagious. Their sadness weighs on you too. To strengthen emotional empathy:

- Watch for Non-Verbal Cues – People often say more with their body language, tone, and expressions than with words.

- Practice Empathic Listening – Don't just hear the words. Tune in to what's underneath them.
- Validate Feelings – Sometimes the best thing you can say is, *"That makes sense,"* or *"I'd feel that way too."*
- Know Your Own Emotions – The more aware you are of your own feelings, the better you'll understand others'.

Compassionate Empathy – *Doing something about it*

This is empathy in action. You feel what someone else feels—and you're moved to help. To strengthen compassionate empathy:

- Practice Small Acts of Kindness – Encouraging words and simple encouraging gestures go a long way.
- Be Responsive – When someone's hurting, don't wait for the perfect plan. Start with presence.
- Create a Caring Culture – Be someone who sets the tone for kindness and support.
- Guide, Don't Fix – Help others navigate their emotions, not by solving them, but by walking alongside them.

Each part of the Empathy Triad adds depth to how we understand and care for others. When you develop all three, you not only build trust— you create stronger relationships wherever you go.

"The quality of your life is the quality of your relationships."
— Tony Robbins

Mastering the Empathy Triad

Once you've developed a strong sense of empathy—when you can understand what others feel, feel it with them, and know when to act—you've stepped into the heart of the Team Builder Role. But that's not the end of the journey. That's where a new kind of challenge begins: **learning to manage the weight of emotions—yours and others.**

Emotions are powerful. They can move us toward connection, or throw us off course. And when you play the Team Builder Role well, you're often the one who notices emotions first. You pick up on shifts in tone, body language, and energy. You feel it all. That's a gift—but it also means you need strategies to stay grounded and protect your emotional balance and your emotional stockpile.

Here are a few simple practices to help you do just that:

Emotional Snapshot

Before entering an emotionally charged situation, pause and take note of how you're feeling—your baseline. After the conversation or event, check in again. Did something shift? Are you carrying emotions that aren't yours? If so, take a moment to release them and return to center.

Take a Break

Big feelings trigger big reactions. And our bodies need time to settle. Strong emotions like anger or grief can take 20 minutes—or more—to process. When things feel overwhelming, step away. Sometimes the very best thing you and others can do in an emotionally charged situation is to take a break.

"Emotions are powerful tools—when we understand them, they stop running the show and start guiding the way."

Left Foot, Right Foot

Bilateral movement—like walking or tapping one foot and then the other—can help calm your nervous system. If you're about to cry or snap, try this small grounding technique. Left foot. Right foot. Even subtle movement helps your brain shift and settle.

Just the Facts

When emotions start to spiral, shift your focus to something factual: the time, the day, something simple and neutral. This pulls your brain out of the emotional zone and back into a calmer state. It works for others too—just make sure you're gentle and respectful.

Set It Down

After an intense moment, name the emotions you're feeling. Ask yourself which ones are yours—and which you might have picked up from someone else. Then picture setting them down. The goal isn't to carry it all. The goal is to respond with care—and then let it go.

"Emotions can get in the way or get you on the way." -Mavis Mazhura

Mastering the Empathy Triad means knowing how to welcome emotions, understand them, respond with care—and then let them go. It's not about carrying everything; it's about staying present without getting overwhelmed. When you do this well, you listen more deeply, stay balanced, and protect yourself from emotional exhaustion.

Have Heart

In the heart of a team, a builder resides,
With empathy & grace, through challenges, guides.
Connecting minds and hearts, in unity they thrive,
With their steady words, trust comes alive.

Through validation's gift, each one gets seen,
In the mirror of respect, where judgment had been.
Advocacy their shield, in the realm of the bold,
Voices are heard, stories are told.

They listen between words, to what hearts say,
Creating safe spaces where fears melt away.
With presence, not pressure, they gently lead,
Planting connection like scattering seed.

They read the room with a quiet grace,
Sensing the tension others might not face.
With empathy sharp and attunement deep,
They hold the space where trust can keep.

They build a space where we want to arrive,
Where trust and purpose together thrive.
Not just a team, but a place to belong—
A rhythm of welcome, a quietly steady song.

So here's to the builders, in teams big and small,
The compassionate leaders, who stand for us all.
Trust weaves its thread, in this tapestry,
In the Team Builder's world, we're free to be.

SUMMARY

The Team Builder Role cares. Of course, all the roles care but only the Team Builder Role leads with the heart. This chapter explores how that's done in real and practical ways. Let's review the contents together. We began with Jea's story, sharing just how powerful this role can be—when it's played well and when it's missing.

Next, we defined the Team Builder Role in both bullet-point and detailed formats, breaking down its key qualities. There is ample 'head' knowledge but this chapter is more than learning the role—it's feeling it.

The practice activities included empathy building, providing safe spaces, and mastering nonverbal communication. If EQ (Emotional Intelligence) wasn't already part of your vocabulary, it will be when you start practicing this role. The Advanced Tips section introduced the Empathy Triad, a powerful framework for truly mastering this role. It has three progressive levels, all centered on 'feelings':

- Understanding how others feel
- Feeling how others feel
- Acting appropriately on those feelings

Yes, the Team Builder works well with others, creates safety, and is the consummate advocate. But at its finest, this role defines genuine trust, the critical ingredient of a great relationship. The Team Builder Role doesn't bring people together—it keeps them together.

"Trust is built when someone is vulnerable and not taken advantage of." -Bob Vanourek

ONE QUICK TIP

If you're eager to start adopting the Team Builder Role, start with this one quick tip: Practice listening.

When someone is speaking, whether it's a colleague discussing a project or a friend sharing a personal story, take a moment to truly focus on what they are saying. Understand their perspective, acknowledge their feelings, and show your support. You can do this by making affirming comments like "I hear you," or asking open ended follow-up questions such as "That must have been so challenging. What did you do next?"

Most importantly, before responding, take a moment to reflect back what you've heard for clarification ("So what you're saying is...") and validate their feelings or perspectives ("That sounds really challenging. I can see why you'd feel that way.")

This small act can make a significant difference, creating a space where people feel heard, understood, and valued. Remember, the journey of a Team Builder begins with showing genuine interest in the experiences and emotions of others.

"Leadership is about empathy. It is about having the ability to relate to and connect with people for the purpose of inspiring and empowering their lives." -Oprah Winfrey

---

ENCOURAGEMENT FROM A TEAM BUILDER

You know, when people ask me about the point of strengthening the Team Builder Role, I want to answer "because it is the best role!" Of course, I don't, because that is not what this role would say. So let me put it in Team Builder words.

It's been such a privilege to feel what people are saying, not just hear the words. The connection with others becomes meaningful, purposeful and at least for me, more interesting.

Playing the Team Builder Role has not just been about work or getting things done by helping others overcome setbacks. It's so much more. It's the only door I know that lets me truly see people. Safety is, of course, paramount and the most important thing I protect. In teams or in families or with friends, there's something profoundly fulfilling about being the thread that weaves individuals into a trusting group. You get to see people at their most real, their most vulnerable—entrusted with their hopes, their fears, and their aspirations.

But more than that, it's the magic that happens when people feel heard and validated.. The spark in their eyes, the newfound determination in their steps—it's like watching life develop right before your eyes. And knowing that you played a part in sparking that change? It's indescribable.

The best part is, these skills, these insights, they don't just apply to others. They've transformed my personal life too. I want to be a better listener, better friend, more empathetic partner, more understanding parent. The Team Builder Role is not just a hat that I wear, it's become a part of who I am.

I want everyone to experience the rewards of this role. When we understand each other better, everything is better. Use this role because it's not just a role, it's a way of life. And it makes life worth living.

EXECUTING THE IMPLEMENTOR ROLE
LIVING TO DO

Are you practical and task-focused?
Do you take immediate action when you see something that needs to be done?
Are you quick to volunteer your help?
Do you get stuff done?!
This is the IMPLEMENTOR ROLE!

WELCOME TO THE IMPLEMENTOR ROLE—THE role that gets things done! Some might argue it's the most essential role, as no project, goal, team, or family functions without it. This is the role that not only creates the to-do list but finishes it. The Implementor executes the plan, fulfills the vision, and ensures the goal is completed. Simply put, if you want to see progress, you need this role.

In this chapter, we'll explore why mastering the Implementor Role is worth the effort. True mastery of the Seven Roles comes from knowing when to step into and out of each one, and the Implementor Role is especially critical—it's the one that turns ideas into reality.

We'll break down the defining characteristics of the Implementor Role, highlighting both its strengths and its limits. Like all roles, it can be overplayed, so we'll also cover strategies to avoid common pitfalls. Along the way, you'll see real-life examples of the Implementor Role in action and gain practical strategies to help you adopt its mindset and master its most essential skill—execution.

While the Implementor Role is essential for progress, not everyone naturally leans into it. Some excel at big-picture thinking, relationship-building, or strategy development but struggle with translating ideas into action. And without execution, even the best ideas remain unfinished potential.

Talia's story is a perfect example. A talented marketing manager, she thrived in roles that required vision and connection. But when it came to following through, she faced a major challenge—one that was beginning to put her job at risk.

Story Part 1: Talia

[Talia: A 30 something marketing manager.] Talia, a 30-something marketing manager, was known for her ability to articulate big ideas and bring people together. Her interpersonal skills and empathy made her a favorite among clients and colleagues alike. She thrived in the Team Builder Role, effortlessly connecting people and fostering collaboration. She also had a strong Prophet Role, allowing her to see long-term vision and inspire others to believe in it.

But there was a noticeable gap in her skill set—she struggled to execute.

Talia's job required her to connect with clients, understand their needs, and develop high-level marketing strategies—all areas where she excelled. But when it came to turning those strategies into concrete action, things fell apart. Her brainstorming sessions energized the team, but without clear follow-through, they often felt directionless and overwhelmed. Her focus on vision and relationships left the daily execution slipping through the cracks.

Now, a major account was at risk. The client had grown frustrated with delays and was losing confidence in the team—and in Talia herself. While her team had conceived a brilliant marketing strategy, progress had stalled. Tasks remained unfinished, deadlines were slipping, and stakeholders were losing patience.

If she didn't figure out how to close the execution gap, Talia wasn't just going to lose a project—she might lose her career momentum, too.

The ability to follow through and finish what's started is the foundation for success for any goal. Let's see how it can help you.

HOW CAN THE IMPLEMENTOR ROLE HELP YOU?

The Implementor Role is indispensable—it's the role that ensures ideas turn into tangible results. While some roles focus on strategy, creativity, or vision, the Implementor Role focuses on practical execution—making sure things actually get done. And that matters:

In Your Relationships

Strong relationships don't just happen—they require follow-through and reliability. The Implementor Role ensures that commitments are kept and practical needs are met, creating a foundation of trust and dependability.

- Keeping your word—showing up when you say you will
- Handling life's logistics—making sure the bills are paid, the car is maintained, the house is stocked
- Taking responsibility—packing the moving boxes, organizing the schedule, following through on shared plans

People who lean into the Implementor Role are the ones others can count on—not just for words, but for action.

In Your Career

In a professional environment, the Implementor is the executor—the one who takes big ideas and turns them into reality. This role makes sure:

- Projects move forward—breaking down goals into actionable steps
- Deliverables are met—hitting deadlines and completing tasks
- Teams stay productive—keeping workflows organized and efficient

The dependability of the Implementor Role often leads to career advancement, as employers and colleagues recognize the value of someone who consistently produces results.

In Your Personal Life

The Implementor Role isn't just about work—it's about getting things done in your own life, too.

- Achieving personal goals—whether it's fitness, learning a skill, or finishing a project
- Building strong habits—following through on routines
- Maintaining discipline—staying focussed on tasks

It's not enough to have an Organizer Role plan, the Implementor Role is needed to execute that plan.

In Your Community

The Implementor Role thrives in volunteer work and community service because these are the people who step up, take on the needs, and see them through.

- Handling event logistics—setting up, organizing, and ensuring smooth execution
- Doing the work others avoid—taking on tedious but necessary tasks

- Bringing ideas to life—ensuring community projects don't just get planned, but actually happen.

Whether in a charity event, local organization, or grassroots movement, Implementors are the backbone of getting things done.

While other six roles dream, strategize, connect, analyze, inspire and innovate, the Implementor executes—making the difference between what could be and what actually is.

IF YOU PLAY THE IMPLEMENTOR ROLE

If you want to get stuff done, jump into the Implementor Role and do it. But this role offers more than just action—it brings structure, dependability, and execution power to any setting. Here are just a few of the many advantages of playing this role:

Proactive Initiator: You see what needs to be done—and you do it. You don't wait for others to point out tasks. Instead, you take initiative and act proactively.

Detail Master: You are detail-oriented, ensuring nothing is overlooked. You take pride in thorough, meticulous work.

Task Strategist: You break down big projects into manageable steps. You excel at taking goals and turning them into logical, clear, actionable to-do lists.

Completion Champion: You prefer to see tasks through from start to finish. You work through each step until the job is done.

Reliability Anchor: You are dependable—others can count on you to follow through. If you say you'll do something, it gets done.

Practical Realist: You focus on the tangible and achievable rather than wishful thinking. You make realistic plans based on available time and resources.

Tenacious Worker: You aren't afraid of tedious or repetitive tasks. You recognize that not every task is exciting, but all work is valuable.

Job Completer: You find satisfaction in completion—checking things off your list feels great.

Team Player: You enjoy contributing to a team working toward a shared goal. You're happy to take on tasks that ensure success for everyone.

Aid Extender: You value service to others and step in when help is needed.

Why This Role Matters

Playing the Implementor Role means being dependable, diligent, and action-oriented. Whether at work, in relationships, or personal projects, you are the driving force that transforms plans into reality and dreams into achievements.

Let's see what happens when Talia includes the Implementor Role to her work flow.

Story Part 2: Talia's Transformation

[Talia: Four months later.] Talia had risen quickly into a leadership role, fueled by her Prophet and Team Builder strengths. She could see the future path and inspire others toward the vision, but the operational side—the step-by-step execution—was where she struggled.

Her wake-up call came when her team struggled to implement a well-conceptualized marketing strategy for a major client. The ideas were brilliant, but progress was slow and disorganized. Frustrated, the client began losing confidence in the team—and in her. It was clear—her lack of execution wasn't just a personal challenge; it was impacting everyone. If she wanted to be a better leader, she needed to strengthen her Implementor Role.

Her first step? Owning the problem.

Talia acknowledged the gaps to her team, taking responsibility for the confusion and lack of execution. She was transparent about the challenges and committed to making real changes—not just for herself, but for the entire team.

But knowing there was a problem wasn't enough. She needed change, she needed an Implementor mindset.

Talia started small. She grabbed a legal pad and pen, and began tracking her daily tasks. Every evening, she evaluated her progress—what worked, what didn't, and where her time was slipping away.

After a week, she expanded the effort, asking her direct reports to do the same. The goal was simple: to uncover the best "get it done" strategies as a team.

Next, she translated her vision into action steps. Using a project management tool, she broke down the high-level ideas into smaller, concrete tasks. Each assignment now had clear deadlines and ownership, creating a structured workflow where everyone knew what to do, when to do it, and why it mattered.

With a clear plan in place, Talia shifted her focus to accountability.

To keep momentum strong, Talia introduced structured, but brief, check-ins. Morning status meetings became a space to highlight wins, address bottlenecks, and clarify next steps. The team, once operating at a relaxed and uncertain pace, began moving with focus and urgency.

As expectations became clearer, morale improved. Instead of feeling overwhelmed or lost, team members felt empowered and productive.

But Talia knew leadership wasn't just about managing tasks—she had to lead by example. Instead of merely delegating, she rolled up her sleeves and worked alongside her team. This hands-on approach helped her understand the execution challenges firsthand.

The transition wasn't easy. At first, she found herself working longer hours than before. But she stuck with it, and over time:

- *Deadlines were met, and the work stayed on track.*
- *Projects moved forward smoothly instead of stalling.*
- *The team felt supported, engaged, and motivated.*
- *The new workflow became second nature—and was even appreciated by the team.*

Talia felt more confident, not just as a visionary leader she already was, but now as an effective executor. Talia's transformation highlights a simple but powerful truth: ideas alone don't create success—execution does. Whether leading a team, managing a household, or pursuing personal goals, the Implementor Role bridges the gap between vision and reality.

But what exactly defines the Implementor Role?

The next section breaks it down, offering a clear definition of the Implementor Role—both in bite-sized bullet points followed by a deeper, more detailed explanation.

"Amateurs sit and wait for inspiration, the rest of us just get up and go to work."—Stephen King

---

THE IMPLEMENTOR BULLETED

*Execution is the difference
between a dream and a reality.*

Proactive Approach: The Implementor Role sees what needs to be done and steps up to get it done, showcasing initiative and drive.

Practical Visionary: The Implementor Role can visualize the steps necessary to complete a task, breaking down complex problems into manageable doable tasks.

Service to Others: The Implementor Role is quick to assist others, eagerly offering support when it can lead to achieving a shared goal. The Implementor Role is quick to say yes to a request for help.

Orderly Execution: This role is characterized by an orderly, methodical, and sequential approach to work, promoting efficiency and quality.

Persistence: The Implementor Role prefers to work on a task from start to finish, showing dedication and commitment to the task at hand.

Attention to Detail: An Implementor is detail-oriented. Nothing falls through the cracks when this role is in play, ensuring all aspects of a task are addressed.

Ask the Implementor: The Implementor Role is practical, reliable, and dependable. If you want it done, ask the Implementor.

Yes, I will: This role doesn't shy away from what others might consider menial or tedious tasks. The focus is on getting the job done and it begins with 'yes, I will do it'.

If this role is unused or underdeveloped:

- Inaction.
- Unfinished tasks.

- Procrastinates.

If this role is overused:

- Difficulty delegating.
- Burnout.
- Over-scheduling.

"Action is the foundational key to all success."
-Pablo Picasso

THE IMPLEMENTOR ROLE DESCRIBED

The Implementor Role is defined by practicality, attention to detail, and a strong work ethic. Implementors are the ones who roll up their sleeves and make things happen, no matter how challenging the task.

Whether at work, in relationships, or personal pursuits, the Implementor Role is the force that turns plans into action. They embody the phrase, *"actions speak louder than words."* They are the doers, the go-getters, the ones who ensure brilliant ideas don't just remain ideas—they become reality.

When the Implementor Role steps in, the focus shifts to what needs to be done and how to do it. They break down complex tasks into clear, manageable steps and execute with precision. Their skill set isn't just for short-term projects—whether tackling a quick task or managing a long-term initiative, Implementors create order out of complexity and ensure steady progress.

Their keen attention to detail cannot be overstated. Implementors dot the i's and cross the t's, noticing nuances that are critical to success. They don't just understand what needs to be done—they grasp the how and can clearly communicate progress at any stage.

Accomplishment fuels the Implementor Role. They are known for their diligence, perseverance, and precision, taking satisfaction in seeing a job through to completion. Short-term wins are especially gratifying, as they can see tangible results from their work.

While they appreciate teamwork, Implementors often prefer to complete their portion independently, ensuring their high standards are met. This isn't due to an inability to delegate, but rather a commitment to quality and confidence in their ability to get things done efficiently and correctly.

Another defining trait of the Implementor Role is their willingness to take on tasks others avoid. Whether the job is tedious, time-consuming, or unglamorous, completion takes priority over preference. Their practical, reliable, and efficient approach makes them an asset to any team or project.

Beyond their own work, Implementors are always ready to help. Their instinctive response to a request for assistance is usually *"yes."* If they can't do it themselves, they'll find the right person who can. Helping others isn't an inconvenience—it's a source of fulfillment, knowing their contributions moved the goal forward.

Finally, orderliness supports the Implementor Role. They function best in a structured environment that allows for focused execution. While they can temporarily set aside order when necessary for the greater goal of productivity, they always return to structure and method—because for them, order isn't just a preference; it's a requirement that supports their role—the role that gets things done.

"Don't watch the clock; do what it does.
Keep going." -Sam Levenson

THE IMPLEMENTOR ROLE PRACTICED

This is the practice section for the Implementor Role with activities and examples. Before we dive into the steps, it's worth noting: **everyone needs more of the Implementor Role.** Unlike other roles that may be used situationally, the Implementor is critical to daily life. Whether at work, at home, or in your personal goals—this is the role that gets things done.

Here, in Implementor-style steps, is how to build up this role:

Step 1: Adopt the Mindset of the Implementor Role

Begin by adopting the mindset of an Implementor, and that starts with a desire to get stuff done. As you read through the suggestions, imagine times when you got things done. What was your mindset? That is the Implementor Role!

Detail Oriented Mindset: Notice everything. Look around. What is being done? Who is doing it? What needs to be done?

Action-Based Perspective: Proactively identify what needs to be done and do it.

Reliable: Do what you say you will do. You can be counted on.

Step 2: Choose an Activity to Practice the Role

The next section contains a range of activities designed to help you embody and practice the Implementor Role. As you put on the mindset of the Implementor Role, you will find the activities align and can help you refine and internalize the important skill of the Implementor Role.

Step 3: Repeat

Consistent practice is key in embodying any role. Keep repeating these activities until they become second nature. Remember, change takes time. Be patient and keep refining your approach.

By regularly practicing these activities, you're nurturing the Implementor Role mindset. With time, you'll find that you more easily play the Implementor Role, making you a more reliable, more efficient, detail-oriented doer.

"I attribute my success to this: I never gave or took any excuse."
-Florence Nightingale

PRACTICAL EXERCISES: IMPLEMENTOR

This is the practice section for the Implementor Role. If you want to build up this role, then do it. Choose an activity and get it done. That is practicing the Implementor Role, Implementor-style.

Orderly Approach: Make a conscious effort to approach all tasks in an orderly, logical way, regardless of size of project.

Vanth, a cybersecurity consultant, helps companies assess risks, strengthen systems, and reduce cyber threats. When a firm experiences a cyberattack, chaos can easily take over—but Vanth remains methodical.

He starts with a structured risk assessment, pinpointing vulnerabilities and prioritizing the most critical threats. Rather than rushing into quick fixes, he follows a step-by-step process, ensuring that each security gap is properly addressed. He then guides the company in implementing long-term system upgrades and compliance measures to prevent future breaches.

By executing an orderly, logical, step-by-step approach, Vanth turns crisis into control.

Task Breakdown: Practice breaking down a complex task into manageable steps.

Harold, a small business owner, dreaded the overwhelming task of filing taxes each year. The paperwork, receipts, and expense tracking always felt like an impossible mountain to climb.

Determined to make the process more manageable, he applied a structured approach. First, he gathered all necessary documents, from receipts to invoices. Next, he categorized expenses into clear sections —supplies, travel, payroll—ensuring nothing was overlooked. He then set aside time to review everything before consulting his accountant, coming prepared with organized records and questions.

Breaking tax filing into clear, actionable steps, transformed a stressful obligation into a simple checklist. Not only can Harold complete this year's taxes with greater ease, he also built a repeatable task list he can use again every year.

Volunteer: Offer your skills and time for a worthwhile project. Every volunteer effort requires Implementors. Whether it's organizing materials, setting up the space, or executing the event. Look for ways to be helpful.

KT is always open to lending a hand. When he learned about the annual kids' event at his church, he discovered that the organizers planned to weeks cutting hundreds of boxes by hand for decorations. Recognizing how tedious and time-consuming this would be, KT offered to help—and he had a die-cutting machine that could do the job more efficiently.

He coordinated with the church to get the designs and materials, ensuring he understood their vision. Over the next few days, he efficiently processed each box with his machine, producing clean, uniform cuts far faster than manual work would allow.

When the event arrived, the designed cut boxes transformed the space into a vibrant wonderland for the kids.

Task Management: Use a task management tool. You can use paper or a digital tool. Setup a checklist style system for daily use.

Isaac, a software engineer, prided himself on getting things done, but lately, the demands of multiple projects had left him struggling to keep up. He didn't need more ideas—he needed a better way to execute the ones already in front of him. That's when he turned to a digital task management tool, not to organize everything again, but to help him get more done.

Instead of feeling overwhelmed by deadlines and competing priorities, Isaac found that using the tool helped him stay focused on what really mattered: completing the priority tasks one by one.

What made the biggest difference was how the tool freed Isaac from constantly worrying about what to do next. With the tasks laid out, he could dive into action without hesitation. The tool became a support system that allowed him to focus on the highest priority 'next' task.

Attention to Detail: Cultivate a habit of noticing details as you work on everyday tasks.

Jules manages equipment maintenance for a small production facility. Every morning, he walks the floor before anyone else arrives, listening for odd sounds and scanning for anything out of place. Most days, everything checks out.

But one Wednesday, something felt off. He paused by a conveyor belt and crouched down. One of the support brackets had a hairline crack near the weld. It wasn't causing a problem yet—but it would.

He flagged it immediately, ordered a replacement part, and scheduled a short repair window that afternoon. The team was surprised—no one had noticed anything wrong.

The next day, the manufacturer confirmed the part had a defect. If Jules hadn't caught it early, the machine would've failed within the week, halting production and costing thousands in delays.

Jules didn't consider what he did as extraordinary. He did what he always does—*paid attention.*

Meeting Deadlines: Set yourself a deadline for a personal project and strive to meet it.

Hadas had always admired runners but never considered herself one —until she decided to sign up for a 5K. She knew that without a clear deadline, she might never commit, so she registered for a race three months away, giving herself a firm goal to work toward.

She started small, alternating between walking and jogging, following a structured training plan to build endurance. Some days were tough —her legs ached, and self-doubt crept in—but she stuck to her schedule, treating each training session as a non-negotiable appointment with herself.

Race day arrived, and as Hadas stood at the starting line, she felt nervous but ready. With every step, she reminded herself of the commitment she had honored over the past three months. Crossing the finish line wasn't just about completing the race—it was proof that setting a deadline and sticking to it had turned a distant goal into a real achievement.

Service to Others: The Implementor Role is quick to assist others, readily offering real support. This role is characterized by a willingness to say yes to requests for help, pitching in and making things happen when they matter the most.

Christina doesn't need to be asked twice when someone needs help. It is her strong Implementor Role instinct to step in, roll up her sleeves, and get to work. When she saw her friend feeling overwhelmed about an upcoming move, Christina immediately saw an opportunity to put her Implementor strengths to good use.

Without hesitation, she got to work—packing boxes, wrapping fragile items, and labeling everything to make unpacking easier. When her friend got distracted sorting through old keepsakes, Christina gently kept things on track, reminding her of their goal and offering to box up sentimental items for later. She even brought extra packing tape and snacks, anticipating what might be needed before anyone asked.

As the hours passed, her steady, task-focused help made all the difference. She kept the energy up, suggesting a playlist to keep things moving, offering quick breaks when needed, and tackling the heaviest lifting without complaint. When the moving truck finally pulled away, her friend turned to her and said, "I couldn't have done this without you."

By the end of the day, Christina's friend was grateful for the physical work—but even more so for her calm, supportive presence.

Quick Helping Hand: Offer help to someone in need. The mindset of this role is task focused. If this is one of your weaker roles, offering 'quick' help is an easy way to step into the action-based style of this role.

When Roberta noticed her elderly neighbor struggling with groceries, she gently asked the neighbor, "Can I help?"

Effective Communication: Practice conveying your plans and task processes clearly to others.

Paul, a dedicated Civil Air Patrol volunteer, was tasked with overseeing a large group of cadets during a critical training exercise. Recognizing the importance of clear communication, he took the time to outline the training objectives and each cadet's responsibilities in a briefing.

To enhance clarity, Paul implemented a visual checklist system that allowed cadets to track their own progress. This ensured task completion while teaching cadets task management.

Paul's approach not only minimized confusion but also fostered a sense of ownership among the cadets. Implementors get more done working together.

Managing Tedious Tasks: Work on completing mundane tasks efficiently. To stay engaged, consider incorporating elements of other roles—for example, use the Luminary Role to make the task more enjoyable or creative.

Jim dreads the tedium of washing his car, but likes it clean. Recently, he turned this chore into a fun activity by involving his kids. The car wash transformed into a playful water fight, making the entire experience enjoyable for everyone involved and resulted in a sparkling clean car.

Starting and Finishing a Task: Choose a project that you can see through from start to finish.

Quinlan is a talented designer, known for his artistic vision and his unique approach to bringing practical ideas to life. When he came up with the concept for a custom car part, he didn't just imagine the finished product—he mapped out a clear, step-by-step process to make it a reality.

Quinlan started by sketching his idea, then methodically developed it into a functional design. He created a detailed task list, from collaborating with others to selecting materials and testing prototypes. He broke the project into manageable steps, ensuring each task was completed before moving on to the next.

Through his task-oriented approach, Quinlan walked his idea down a path from a Prophet Role concept to an Implementor Role completion; ready for delivery.

Short-term Planning: Try planning your week in advance with specific doable, daily goals. List making is a basic, necessary skill for the Implementor Role.

Anna settles into her cozy kitchen with a cup of tea. She knows that taking a little time to create her grocery list can make a big difference.

As she flips through her Organizer Role planner, Anna begins by reviewing her schedule. She notes the days she'll be busy with work commitments and social events.

Next, Anna makes a list of healthy recipes she wants to try, considering seasonal ingredients and her family's preferences. She decides on a mix of quick meals for hectic days and a few more elaborate dishes for evenings when she can spend time cooking. After selecting her recipes, she writes down the ingredients she needs.

With her meal plan in hand, Anna heads to the grocery store. Armed with a detailed shopping list, she moves efficiently through the aisles, enjoying the process rather than feeling rushed.

Actively Resist Procrastination: Identify a task you've been putting off and complete it.

For months, Ardell wanted to paint the living room but was unable to decide on the perfect color. Finally, one Saturday, she resolved to take action and set a goal to complete the task by the end of the weekend.

After selecting a warm, inviting hue, she cleared the room and prepped the walls. As she applied the first coat of paint, Ardell felt motivated by the transformation unfolding before her eyes. By the time she finished the second coat, the space was brighter and more welcoming than she had imagined.

Stepping back to admire her work, she felt a surge of accomplishment. Not only had she selected exactly the right paint, she had revitalized her home.

Task Prioritization: Learn to prioritize tasks based on urgency. Then, do them.

Tom had several ranch tasks to tackle over the weekend: fixing a broken fence, ordering more hay, and repairing a gate. He prioritized the tasks and got to work. The broken fence took top priority—it needed immediate attention to keep the animals secure. Ordering more hay and fixing the gate, were next. Tom methodically worked through the list, focusing on the most pressing tasks first before moving on to the rest.

By the end of the weekend, Tom had completed everything on his list in order of importance.

The Implementor Role is the "get it done" role—the one you rely on when results matter. A great goal is to notice when and how often you step into this role. Do you rely on it too much, getting caught up in busywork? Or too little, over-preparing or procrastinating instead of taking action?

Either way, awareness is the first step. By recognizing your patterns, you can learn to balance efficiency with strategy. The Implementor Role does not waste time. They get stuff done. And, most likely, we could all use this role…more.

Nothing is more satisfying than a job well done.

ADVANCED TIPS FOR PLAYING THE IMPLEMENTOR ROLE

The greatest strength of the Implementor Role lies in its ability to transform ideas into actions with results. Those who play this role are practical, dependable, and have an eagle eye for details. The focus on action, coupled with a dedication to providing dependable results, makes it a valuable role for anyone, anytime.

But, like all roles, there can be downsides if we overplay it. Let's explore a couple potential pitfalls and how to avoid or overcome them.

I Can Do It All!

It can be tempting to take on all tasks yourself because you know you'll get the job done. However, this can quickly end in burnout. It can also lead to doing tasks that others should be doing for themselves. There is a fine line between enabling others and enabling others to do what belongs to them. Finding and honoring that line is necessary to playing this role and critical if this is your goto role.

Speak Up: This is probably the greatest challenge for those who regularly favor this role. If the goal of the role is to get work done, speaking up can feel like a wrench in the works of productivity. Maybe the deadline is too ambitious, maybe the needed materials are not available, maybe you need a new skill; whatever the issue, the tendency for the Implementor is to power through. Voicing your concerns when tasks aren't adequately supported is essential. Learning to speak up sooner rather than later both protects this role and greatly enhances the results that can be accomplished. Speak up.

Asking for Help: For those strong in the Implementor Role, it's natural to believe that if you want a job done right, it's easiest to do it yourself. But when it comes to big goals, help isn't just useful—it's essential. While it may be tempting to shoulder tasks independently, this can quickly lead to burnout. More importantly, it can deny others the chance to grow or contribute.

The key is to ask for help intentionally—be specific in your requests and don't wait until it's a crisis. There is a big difference between helping others and enabling them to avoid responsibility. Learning to navigate that distinction is a skill every strong Implementor must develop.

While asking for help is a necessary skill in the Implementor Role, true efficiency comes from taking it a step further and mastering delegation. Delegation isn't just about offloading tasks; it's about leveraging the Implementor Role's "get it done" mindset to empower others to take action effectively.

So, how do you delegate in a way that maintains the get it done skill of the Implementor Role? Let's explore that in the next section.

Smart Delegation Implementor Style

Delegation is about getting the job done, but it's also about developing the capabilities of others. Effective delegation maximizes efficiency while also encouraging growth, allowing team members, family, or volunteers to build confidence and new skills.

Unlike simply asking for help, delegation involves assigned or assumed authority tied to a goal or team effort. A team manager has assigned authority over their team, a parent has assumed responsibility for their child, and a volunteer organization operates within a structured management system—each creating a clear role for directing tasks.

Effective delegation isn't just about offloading work—it's about leveraging the strengths of others to achieve the best results. Whether in a workplace, volunteer setting, or personal responsibilities, the Implementor Role excels when it transforms independent action into coordinated execution.

Delegation applies across many areas of life, including community leadership, household management, entrepreneurship, education, and collaborative projects. Whether organizing an event, managing a team, running a household, or mentoring others, strong delegation ensures tasks are completed efficiently while also helping others develop the ability to contribute at a higher level.

How to Delegate Effectively Using the Implementor Role Perspective

1. Define Your Role and Responsibilities

Before delegating, clarify what belongs to you. Whether in a workplace, family, or volunteer setting, determine:

- *What outcome or goal am I responsible for?*
- *What authority or decision-making power do I have?*
- *Am I responsible for overseeing the process, the final result, or both?*

2. Identify Who Can Contribute

Delegation works best when tasks are distributed to the right people based on their skills, availability, and role. Consider:

- *Who is available to contribute?*
- *What are their strengths or areas for growth?*
- *How much oversight or guidance will they need?*

3. Break Down the Work Into Manageable Pieces

Instead of assigning broad tasks, break them into clear, actionable steps. This ensures efficiency and helps avoid confusion.

- *What are the key steps to completing this task?*
- *Which parts require specialized skills, and which are simple but time-consuming?*

4. Assign Tasks with Clarity and Ownership

Be clear and specific about expectations, deadlines, and outcomes. Delegation works best when people understand not just what to do, but why it matters.

- *What is the expected result?*
- *What deadlines or milestones should be met?*
- *Does the person understand how their task contributes to the bigger picture?*

5. Equip and Empower

Delegation isn't about simply handing off work and hoping for the best—it's about ensuring others have what they need to succeed. Provide the right tools, resources, and initial support, then step back.

- *Have I provided the necessary tools and information upfront?*
- *Do they feel confident tackling this task, or do they need more support?*
- *Am I encouraging problem-solving rather than just giving instructions?*

By equipping people with knowledge, authority, and trust, Implementors create capable and confident contributors who can take ownership of tasks rather than just following orders.

6. Provide Support Without Micromanaging

The Implementor Role thrives on getting things done, but effective delegation requires stepping back. Offer resources, guidance, and check-ins while still allowing autonomy.

- *Do they have the tools and information they need?*
- *Is there an obstacle I can help remove to ensure progress?*
- *Am I checking in at key moments, or am I hovering?*

- *Am I providing support, or am I unintentionally taking the task back?*

7. Reinforce and Recognize Contributions

Delegation isn't just about efficiency—it's also about developing others and building momentum for future collaboration. Acknowledge contributions and highlight how their work impacts the bigger goal.

- *How did it go?*
- *Did they meet expectations or go beyond?*
- *Are they ready for more responsibility?*
- *How can I show appreciation in a way that encourages continued engagement?*

Doing More... Together

By integrating these strategies, the Implementor Role moves beyond simply getting things done to leading others in execution. Whether at home, in the workplace, or within a community, effective delegation shares the workload, fosters collaboration, and ensures efficiency—all while helping others grow.

Delegation isn't just about productivity; it's about building momentum, distributing responsibility, and ensuring that work is reliably completed. When done well, it allows Implementors to maximize efficiency, empower others, and create an environment where progress keeps moving forward.

"It is better to lead from behind and to put others in front, especially when you celebrate victory when nice things occur. You take the front line when there is danger. Then people will appreciate your leadership." -Nelson Mandela

Can You See Me?

The Implementor Role is often a work-in-the-background kind of role—essential for getting things done but sometimes overlooked. Those who play this role well tend to focus on execution over recognition, leading to their efforts being under-appreciated or even taken for granted.

While staying behind the scenes can feel natural, visibility matters—not for ego, but for recognition, career growth, and ensuring that contributions are valued. Here are some strategies to opt to be seen while staying true to the Implementor Role's strengths.

Advocate for Yourself

People who strongly play the Implementor Role often minimize their work by saying things like *"I helped..."* or *"I was part of..."* instead of fully owning their contributions. While this instinct comes from humility and teamwork, it can lead to others overlooking the full extent of their efforts.

Don't be afraid to speak directly about what you accomplished. It's not about bragging—it's about ensuring your contributions are acknowledged and that others understand the work that goes into execution.

- Work Example: Instead of saying, *"I helped with the project,"* say, *"I structured the timeline so we met all deadlines."*
- Volunteering Example: Instead of saying, *"I was part of the fundraiser,"* say, *"I managed the check-in table, ensuring 200 guests got in smoothly and efficiently."*
- Parenting Example: Instead of saying, *"I helped get the kids*

to practice," say, *"I coordinated our family schedule so each child made it to their activities without conflicts."*

This subtle shift in language clarifies the impact of your role and makes it easier for others to see and appreciate the value you bring.

Request Feedback

Regularly asking for feedback does two things; it reinforces your presence and reminds others of your contributions and it helps you refine your role and improve efficiency.

- Work Example: *"Is the new workflow I set up helping everyone stay on track?"*
- Volunteering Example: *"Would a different layout for the food station make next year's event run more smoothly?"*
- Parenting Example: *"Is our morning routine working for everyone, or is there something we should adjust?"*

Work on Visibility

Help others see the work behind the work. The more transparent you are about your process, the more your efforts are understood and valued.

- Work Example: Instead of just submitting a completed report, briefly mention how you streamlined the data collection.
- Volunteering Example: Instead of just showing up with assembled gift baskets, share how you found a way to get donated supplies, saving the organization money.
- Parenting Example: Instead of quietly handling all the logistics for a family vacation, mention how you researched deals and mapped out the route.

People Who Need People

For those who strongly play the Implementor Role, personal interactions and leadership responsibilities can feel like distractions from the "real work." However, cultivating relationships and demonstrating leadership are essential to fully mastering the effectiveness of this role.

"Networking" is Not a Bad Word: Implementors often focus on tasks and processes, sometimes missing the importance of relationships. To foster a better connection with others:

- Work Example: Get to know how your coworkers prefer to work—it helps prevent misunderstandings and improves collaboration.
- Volunteering Example: Learn about why other volunteers are involved—this builds camaraderie and might help you recruit more people for future efforts.
- Parenting Example: Take time to understand what motivates your kids—some may respond better to structure, while others thrive on independence.

Lean in to Leadership: Volunteering for leadership roles can spotlight your capabilities and show that the Implementor Role is essential for effective execution.

- Work Example: Offer to coordinate workflows, streamline processes, or mentor others in task execution.
- Volunteering Example: Step up to manage event logistics or train new volunteers—this highlights your ability to make things run smoothly.
- Parenting Example: Show leadership by teaching kids to manage their own tasks—delegate small responsibilities and help them build confidence in execution.

Communicate Regularly and Effectively: Keeping others informed ensures your hard work isn't overlooked.

- Work Example: *"The office supply orders are now on an automated schedule, so we won't run out unexpectedly."*
- Volunteering Example: *"I'll be at the park cleanup early setting up trash stations—if you need anything, let me know!"*
- Parenting Example: *"I put together a shared grocery list in an app so we can all add what we need and avoid multiple trips."*

Being Seen Without Seeking the Spotlight

Making your work visible isn't about self-promotion—it's about ensuring that the value you bring is recognized, respected, and rewarded. By choosing when and how to highlight your contributions, you gain influence without stepping away from what makes the Implementor Role so effective—getting things done.

"Execution… is the missing link between aspirations and results." -Bossidy

The greatest strength of the Implementor Role lies in its ability to transform ideas into concrete actions and outcomes. Those who play this role well are practical, dependable, and detail-oriented, ensuring that tasks move forward and goals are achieved. However, like all roles, leaning too heavily on its strengths can create challenges.

Ultimately, the Implementor Role effectiveness explodes when execution is paired with a 'get it done' leadership style. By combining efficiency, communication, and delegation, Implementors not only get things done but empower others to execute at their highest potential. Go Implementor.

"Start where you are. Use what you have. Do what you can."
— *Arthur Ashe*

Action Speaks

In a world of dreams, the Implementor stands tall,
With practical thoughts and hands that enthrall.
Seeing tasks to do, both great and small,
For ideas are nothing, without action after all.

With a list in hand and a goal in sight,
The Implementor works from morning till night.
No task too menial, no work too rough,
They persevere, when the going gets tough.

They carry the plans, the steps, the how,
Not someday dreams—but action now.
Where others stall or overthink,
The Implementor builds the missing link.

When progress halts or teams lose steam,
They steady the course and lift the dream.
For every vision, spark, or scheme—
It's the Implementor who makes it seen.

A practical visionary, they chart the course,
Breaking complex into simple, with gentle force.
To those in need, they extend their hand,
A service to others, helping dreams to land.

Checking off tasks, as each day unfolds,
Turning dreams into reality, as the story is told.
To the dreamers and thinkers, they quietly say,
"Dreams are great, but let's bring them to life today."

SUMMARY

In this chapter, we've worked through the Implementor Role, a critical role for absolutely everyone because it focuses on getting things done. Let's summarize the information and see what you've accomplished. Check off what you have completed…like an Implementor.

☐ **Understanding the Implementor Role** – You learned what it means to be the doer, the one who steps up, takes action, and follows through.

☐ **Practicing the role** – You worked through hands-on exercises designed to sharpen your efficiency, reliability, and attention to detail.

☐ **Recognizing pitfalls** – You explored the risks of overusing this role, such as burnout, being undervalued, or missing the big picture. You also identified what happens when this role is underused, leading to procrastination, disorganization, and unfinished tasks.

☐ **Reviewing real-world examples** – You saw how Implementors make a difference, from boosting team productivity to keeping volunteer organizations running smoothly to simply being helpful.

☐ **I Can Do It All! (Or Can I?)** – You learned that while it's tempting to take on everything yourself, this often leads to burnout and doing tasks that should belong to others. Knowing when to step back is just as important as stepping up.

☐ **Speaking Up for What's Needed** – You discovered that powering through isn't always the best strategy. Sometimes, deadlines are unrealistic, resources are missing, or a new skill is required. Learning to speak up early prevents problems.

☐ **Asking for Help the Right Way** – You explored the fine line between helping others and enabling them.

☐ **Smart Delegation, Implementor Style** – You learned that delegation isn't about offloading work—it's about leveraging strengths and fostering growth.

☐ **Final Takeaway** — The Implementor Role is the difference between dreaming and achieving.

☐ **Mission Complete** – You've checked off every box. Now it's time to do what Implementors do best—get things done!

"The future depends on what you do today." -Mahatma Gandhi

ONE QUICK TIP

A standout trait of the Implementor Role is a readiness to step up and get things done. An Implementor Role player is often the first to notice when something needs to be done. This "jump in" trait is what makes the Implementor Role so valuable—they're the ones you can always rely on to roll up their sleeves and get to work. If you're usually hesitant to take initiative, start cultivating a "can do" attitude.

Look around and identify what needs to be done and if you can help then move quickly to do it. This might look like being the first to say yes when help is needed or better yet, being proactive: noticing what needs to be done and doing it.

"The way to get started is to quit talking and begin doing."
-Walt Disney

INITIATING THE IMPLEMENTOR ROLE

As someone who often plays the Implementor Role, I can say with certainty that this approach is the driving force behind my getting things done. It's the essential link between a grand idea and a finished product, the engine that powers my goals.

I relish turning lofty ideas into practical steps. There's a unique satisfaction that comes with seeing a task through from start to finish. This satisfaction fuels my determination, making even the most mind-boggling projects become achievable.

My approach is methodical, and some might even call it meticulous. I break down long-term goals into smaller, manageable tasks. And these tasks aren't just arbitrarily created. I think about them, order them, and make sure each step leads logically to the next step.

And it's not just about ticking boxes. My attention to detail ensures that things don't fall through the cracks. I am that safety net, catching any overlooked aspects that might otherwise compromise our success.

But what I truly love about playing the Implementor Role is its universality. Whether it's a personal goal, a work project, or a community initiative, the role fits. I can always choose to step up to meet practical needs, making dreams a reality in every part of my life.

For me, it's more than just getting the job done. It's about transforming the realm of what's possible into the world of what is. I like to make things happen, to know I was a part of turning what was just a dream into something real. So, for anyone wondering why things get done, join in with the Implementors. We're the ones turning the gears behind the scenes.

Turn your plans into actions. Go us!

THINKING LIKE THE CONCEPTUALIZER ROLE
LIVING THOUGHTFULLY

Are you data-focused in your decision-making?
Do you seek out new knowledge and
understanding of complex issues?
Are you curious about the world around you?
Do you share what you learn with others?
This is the CONCEPTUALIZER ROLE!

THIS IS the role of logic, analysis, and discovery—the one that seeks to understand, explain, and validate. If the Implementor builds and the Luminary inspires, the Conceptualizer questions, investigates, and connects ideas.

In this chapter, we'll break down the key characteristics, strengths, and challenges of the Conceptualizer Role. Like a professor or scientist, those who play this role excel at examining details, weighing options, and conducting deep research before drawing conclusions. Their dedication to understanding often makes them experts in their field, the ones people turn to for insight and clarity.

The Conceptualizer Role is part detective, part problem-solver—constantly seeking answers, testing ideas, and refining theories until every puzzle piece fits perfectly. Curiosity isn't just an asset in this role—it's the fuel that drives progress.

Ready to think deeply, question boldly, and uncover hidden connections? Then you're ready to step into the Conceptualizer Role.

But what happens when someone needs this role but doesn't play it? Let's take a look at Jer, someone who could benefit from stepping into the Conceptualizer Role.

Story Part 1: Jer

[Jer: A 30 something analyst.] Meet Jer, a dynamic sales director at a fast-paced tech company. Charismatic and effortlessly persuasive, Jer had built his career on his ability to excite and inspire. His natural Luminary and Team Builder strengths made him an exceptional motivator, rallying teams and clients alike. However, there was one role he often overlooked—the Conceptualizer.

When the company prepared to launch a groundbreaking software solution, Jer jumped in as he always did—leading with enthusiasm, stirring excitement, and confidently pitching to clients. He assumed his energy and storytelling skills would carry the presentation, as they always had.

At first, it worked. The room was engaged, nodding along, eager to hear more.

Then came the questions.

A potential client asked how the software handled data encryption. Another wanted to know how it compared to a rival product. Jer hesitated. He had memorized the marketing materials, but he hadn't dug into the technical aspects or thoroughly researched the competition. His usual confidence wavered. He stumbled over explanations, giving vague, surface-level answers. Clients weren't convinced.

Worse, his team noticed. Their once high-energy leader was now fumbling, and morale dipped. His sales strategy lacked the necessary depth, and objections from potential buyers went unanswered.

As feedback from lost sales piled up, Jer realized something critical: charisma alone wasn't enough. If he wanted to lead effectively and close deals, he needed to step into the Conceptualizer Role.

HOW CAN THE CONCEPTUALIZER ROLE HELP YOU?

The Conceptualizer Role is a powerful tool in every aspect of life. Whether tackling personal goals, professional challenges, or social interactions, stepping into this role sharpens your ability to understand, communicate, and solve problems.

In Relationships: Understanding and Explaining

The Conceptualizer Role enhances your ability to listen, process, and articulate ideas clearly. It allows you to dig deeper—whether that's making sense of a complicated news topic, discussing a social issue with friends, or being the one who can explain a tricky concept at a dinner party.

For example, if a friend is struggling with a tough decision, you might research options, break down the pros and cons, and help them make sense of their choices. Conceptualizers don't just offer advice—they equip others with clarity.

In Your Career: Analyzing, Innovating, and Teaching

Professionally, this role sets you apart by giving you the ability to grasp complex systems, spot inefficiencies, and communicate insights. Whether it's troubleshooting a process, identifying industry trends, or simplifying technical concepts for a team, Conceptualizers make sense of big ideas and break them down for others.

For instance, if your company adopts new software, you might be the one who learns it inside and out, then teaches your colleagues how to use it effectively. This role positions you as the go-to person for insight and innovation.

In Your Personal Life: Making Smarter Decisions

At a personal level, the Conceptualizer Role helps you gather information, weigh options, and make informed choices. Whether planning your financial future, improving your health, or starting a new hobby, this role keeps you focused on facts rather than assumptions.

For example, if you're considering a new diet, instead of following trends blindly, you'd research different approaches, analyze their impact, and choose the best fit for your needs. Conceptualizers don't just act—they act with knowledge.

Why This Role Matters

At its core, the Conceptualizer Role helps you make sense of the world. It allows you to navigate uncertainty, think critically, and communicate with confidence. Whether you're deciphering information, guiding a team, or solving personal challenges, playing this role gives you the tools to succeed in any situation.

IF YOU PLAY THE CONCEPTUALIZER ROLE

The Conceptualizer Role seeks the facts. Playing this role well requires taking the time to research, think and understand. The result is greater clarity and much more. Here is what you gain when using this role.

Insightful Analyst: You thrive on deep dives into topics, seeking thorough, fact-based understanding and valuing data-informed decisions.

Great Debater: You appreciate the power of well-supported arguments.

Inquisitive Scholar: You have an unending quest for knowledge, continually learning and asking challenging questions to expand understanding.

Reflective Intellectual: You value truth and accuracy, often taking time to reflect deeply and dissect complex systems and concepts.

Pattern Recognizer: You have a talent for identifying patterns and trends, ensuring that your strategies and decisions consider a wide range of factors.

Knowledge Sharer: You enjoy discussing ideas and theories. You can explain things in detail, and are willing to do so. You communicate complex ideas with patience.

Comprehension Guardian: You ensure understanding is complete and accurate, often becoming engrossed in the process of gaining more information.

Decision Rationalizer: You're the go-to for understanding the rationale behind decisions, providing detailed explanations that ensure clarity.

Learning Enthusiast: You never settle for what you already know. You're the one who can answer the questions that start with, "What?" and "How?" and you enjoy researching and presenting data to back up your explanations.

The Expert: You are or aim to be an expert in your field, providing insightful answers to strategic questions and backing up explanations with solid research and understanding.

Story Part 2: Jer

Jer quickly realized he was missing crucial information—not just about the product, but about the market, competition, and customer concerns. If he didn't close this knowledge gap, the product launch—and his credibility—were at risk.

Determined to turn things around, he stepped fully into the Conceptualizer Role. He immersed himself in the technical details, sitting down with the developers and asking precise questions. He didn't just listen—he took notes, challenged assumptions, and made sure he could explain every feature in simple, compelling terms.

But understanding the product wasn't enough. Jer studied the competition—analyzing features, pricing, and customer reviews to identify gaps and advantages. He combed through client feedback, pinpointing patterns in objections and unmet needs.

Armed with this deeper knowledge, Jer transformed from a salesperson into a strategist and teacher. He gathered his team and broke everything down:

- What made their software unique and how to articulate it.
- Where competitors fell short and how to highlight their advantage.
- How to anticipate and overcome objections with confidence and clarity.

With a refined sales strategy, Jer's team shifted from enthusiasm to expertise. Their pitches became more confident, more precise, and more persuasive. Instead of just selling a product, they were now educating clients, addressing concerns before they arose, and positioning themselves as trusted advisors.

The results spoke for themselves. Sales gained traction, client interest soared, and the product launch rebounded. But beyond that, Jer had transformed—not just as a salesperson, but as a leader. His willingness to step into the Conceptualizer Role had not only salvaged the launch but elevated his team, his company, and himself.

> "Somewhere, something incredible is waiting to be known."
> -Carl Sagan

THE CONCEPTUALIZER ROLE BULLETED

*Expertise is not just knowledge,
but a commitment to understanding.*

Deep Thinkers: Conceptualizers understand the value of taking time to reflect and think deeply.

Investigative: Often undertake deep dives to investigate and research.

Experts: Tend to be an expert in their field. Others seek out what they know.

Data-Driven: Value facts and base decisions on solid evidence.

Inquisitive: A propensity for asking probing and challenging questions.

Instructional: Explain complexities in an easy-to-understand way.

Lifelong Learners: Conceptualizers are naturally curious and have a strong desire for continuous learning and intellectual growth.

Complexity Dissector: They seek to detangle a complex system, meticulously dissecting for better understanding.

Systematic Approach: They approach problems and tasks systematically, thoroughly analyzing every facet before drawing conclusions or making decisions.

Value Accuracy: They place high importance on accuracy and truth, striving to ensure that their assertions are backed by reliable data.

If this role is unused or underdeveloped:

- Decisions are made without supporting data.
- Information is not adequately shared.
- Historical information is discounted or ignored.

If this role is overused:

- Risk-averse.
- Offers too much information.
- Analysis paralysis.

"The task of education is not to teach subjects but to teach the individual how to think." -Jules Payot

THE CONCEPTUALIZER ROLE DESCRIBED

The Conceptualizer Role is defined by a deep, investigative mindset. Those who embody this role have a keen drive to understand, often immersing themselves in research to decipher complex problems and ideas. Their intellectual curiosity pushes them to seek knowledge continuously, positioning them as experts in their field—a role they maintain through constant learning and refinement.

Driven by facts and data, Conceptualizers ground their ideas and decisions in evidence rather than assumptions or emotions. They value accuracy and truth, ensuring their conclusions are backed by logical reasoning and reliable sources. Their commitment to fact-checking and thorough analysis results in a structured, systematic approach to solving problems. They meticulously dissect, question, and verify before drawing conclusions, always striving for clarity and precision.

Conceptualizers seek to untangle complexity. They break down intricate systems into understandable elements, making sense of patterns, trends, and structures that others might overlook. This ability allows them to project future outcomes, anticipate challenges, and refine strategies with a strong analytical foundation.

But knowledge alone isn't enough—they are also communicators and educators. The Conceptualizer Role is defined not just by gathering information but by translating it into something useful and accessible. They patiently explain complex ideas, ensuring others grasp the concepts rather than simply receiving raw data. Their ability to bridge knowledge gaps makes them valuable mentors, teachers, and thought leaders.

Conceptualizers prioritize consistency and predictability. They think before they act, favoring well-researched plans over impulsive decisions. They are the ones asking the tough questions, challenging ideas, and ensuring proof of concept before moving forward.

At its core, the Conceptualizer Role is fueled by curiosity, deep thinking, and a relentless pursuit of knowledge. These individuals understand the power of reflection, taking time to explore ideas, question assumptions, and uncover deeper truths. When balanced, this role provides a strong foundation for insight, discovery, and innovation—ensuring that what is known today leads to better decisions for tomorrow.

THE CONCEPTUALIZER ROLE PRACTICED

In the following section, a three-step process is outlined to help you better adopt and practice the Conceptualizer Role. This process starts with acquiring the mindset of a Conceptualizer.

A mindset is a choice. It refers to a collection of attitudes and approaches that shapes how an individual perceives and interacts with the world. Adopting a new mindset is like training your brain to approach situations and respond to challenges in new, more effective ways. By deliberately practicing new ways of thinking and behaving, we can form new neural pathways in our brains that help us to sustain these new approaches.

Step 1: Adopt the Conceptualizer's Mindset

To genuinely step into the Conceptualizer Role, you'll need to internalize a specific investigative mindset. This includes:

• **Deep Thinking**: You understand the value of taking time to reflect and think.

• **Investigative**: You engage in deep dives to investigate and research interesting, relevant topics.

• **Expert**: You strive to be an expert.

• **Data-Driven**: You value facts and seek to base decisions on solid evidence.

- **Instructional**: You explain to others what you have learned in an easy-to-understand and logical way.

- **Systematic Approach**: You approach problems and tasks systematically, thoroughly analyzing every facet before drawing conclusions or making decisions.

Once you understand these mindset traits, you're ready to move onto the next step.

Step 2: Choose an Activity to Practice the Role

Next, you'll choose from a series of activities designed to help you practice the Conceptualizer Role. The activities align with the mindset of a Conceptualizer, helping you learn the skills and methods to practice and develop it.

You can choose a single mindset trait and pair it with an activity if you don't play this role very often. Or if you are already strong in this role, focus on the areas that would benefit from practice to take your role play to the next level.

Embracing this role means adopting a way of thinking that values questions as much as answers, sees challenges as opportunities for learning, and understands that behind every piece of data lies a story waiting to be told. For the Conceptualizer Role, the world is a vast puzzle where each piece, no matter how small or obscure, is essential to the bigger picture.

Step 3: Repeat

Repeat the chosen activities consistently. This repetition will help you incorporate the Conceptualizer Role into your everyday behavior. The more you practice, the more comfortable and proficient you'll become at fulfilling the role.

Remember, adopting a new mindset is a journey of personal growth and transformation. It won't happen overnight, but with persistence, the Conceptualizer Role mindset will eventually become an integral part of your thought patterns and behaviors, enriching both your professional and personal life in profound ways.

"The greatest enemy of knowledge is not ignorance, it is the illusion of knowledge." -Stephen Hawking

---

PRACTICAL EXERCISES: CONCEPTUALIZER

This is the learning section for the Conceptualizer Role. If you want to expand this role, read through this section and *think* about which activities would stretch your existing skillset and match your current goals.

Deep Diving Exercise: Choose a topic you know little about and commit to researching it thoroughly.

When Craig, a software developer, was asked to join a project exploring cryptocurrency integration, he realized he didn't know enough to contribute with confidence. Instead of skimming the basics, he dove in. He spent evenings reading white papers, watching tutorials, and tracing how blockchain technology actually worked.

Within a month, Craig had more than just a better understanding—he had real insight. He became the team's go-to person for anticipating how crypto might affect the platform's architecture and user experience. What started as a knowledge gap became a place of expertise, all because he was willing to go deep.

Fact-Checking Practice: Whenever you read a piece of news or an article, take the time to fact-check the information presented.

Sarah, a marketing executive, found errors in recent press releases. In

order to prevent this from occurring again, she took on checking them herself, cross-referencing the content with other reliable sources.

Questioning Exercise: Make a point to ask probing questions. This will help you understand the topic better and also encourage others to think more deeply.

Kevin's natural curiosity leads him to ask questions that bring meaningful insights. At work, he notices inefficiencies. Instead of proposing immediate fixes, he asks probing questions like, "How are we doing this now?" and "What could simplify this?" His questions spark discussions, ultimately leading to more streamlined, effective processes.

At home, Kevin takes the same approach, asking open-ended questions that help his family see different perspectives. His skill as a Conceptualizer—asking questions that prompt deeper thinking—creates positive change in both his personal and his professional life.

Teaching Exercise: Explain a complex topic to someone. This will not only test your understanding of the subject but also enhance your communication skills.

Tim has a remarkable ability to break down complex concepts into simple, relatable terms. Whether he is speaking to colleagues, clients, or curious friends, Tim finds ways to explain difficult ideas using analogies and everyday examples.

His ability to simplify complex information not only helps others grasp difficult topics but also deepens Tim's own understanding, proving that teaching and learning go hand in hand.

Data Analysis Practice: Look at information from the news, or from your personal life or at your work or the stock market and analyze it. Look for trends and patterns and make predictions based on your observations. Keep track of this practice to see how your predictions worked out and what would have made the predictions more accurate.

Jake, a sales analyst, wanted to understand how his division could better meet market demand. He began analyzing regional sales data, looking for patterns and trends that others had overlooked.

Over time, his insights revealed imbalances—some teams were overextended in fast-growing regions, while others had more resources than demand. He presented a proposal to restructure the sales teams to better align with market sizes and potential.

Thanks to his analysis, the division made strategic adjustments that improved both efficiency and performance. Jake's ability to turn raw data into clear, actionable insight made a lasting impact on the way the team operated.

Deep Reflection Exercise: Set aside time each day to reflect on what you have learned. This helps in better assimilation of knowledge while holding you accountable to find things to learn.

Erika wanted to start her own business, but she quickly realized that passion alone wasn't enough—there was a steep learning curve ahead. Each day brought new challenges: business licenses, website platforms, pricing models, branding decisions.

To stay grounded and make real progress, she committed to a daily reflection habit. Each evening, Erika sat down and asked herself two questions: What did I learn today? and What do I still need to figure out? Sometimes she jotted down new marketing terms she had researched; other times, she reflected on where she was and where she still needed to go.

She created space to think—and in that space, clarity grew.

Accuracy Focus Practice: When writing or speaking, ensure that your statements are accurate and based on facts.

Nicole, an executive business partner, practices this daily in her role. She carefully documents key points from meetings and conversations, consistently cross-checking what she's heard with relevant data and evidence.

Her careful approach ensures that her communications with her team and stakeholders is clear, reliable, and trustworthy.

Complexity Dissecting Exercise: Choose a complex system or process and dissect it into its component parts. Learn as much as you can about the system.

Cora, an artist, grew tired of not understanding the repairs that were needed for her car. She spent a week doing a deep dive into car mechanics and specifically, her car model. The next time she took her car in, she not only understood what they were saying and planning on doing, she was able to reasonably decide what was needed and when.

A side benefit, which was actually more impactful for her, was that she felt respected in the interchange.

Learning Practice: Try to learn something new every day.

Dr. Louise is always seeking knowledge, and not just within her medical specialty. Every day, she finds time to explore something new, whether reading the latest research, attending virtual conferences, or listening to podcasts during her commute or workouts.

From advancements in technology to insights on art and culture, Dr. Louise knows that learning across diverse fields deepens her expertise and offers fresh perspectives to her medical practice. It also has the added benefit of inspiring others with the information she shares.

By committing to daily learning, Dr. Louise feels more connected and engaged with the world around her.

Logical Reasoning Practice: Practice solving logical reasoning problems. This can be done using puzzles or logic-based games.

Abraham, a lawyer, plays a brain-exercising app as part of his preparation for court cases. He has found that a mental challenge warmup helps him to think more clearly in the moment.

Sharing Info Patiently: Explain a complex topic to someone without getting impatient.

Kyle, a doctor known for both his depth of knowledge and calming presence, was called in on a particularly complicated case. Multiple specialists had weighed in, but the diagnosis and next steps remained unclear.

After reviewing the details, Dr. Kyle offered a clear path forward—grounded in evidence, but delivered without jargon. He sat with the patient and their family, walking through the condition, the reasoning behind his recommendation, and what to expect next. As understanding took hold, so did a sense of relief.

Dr. Kyle's strength isn't just in what he knows—it's in how he shares it. With clarity, confidence, and patience, he helps people make sense of complexity and move forward with confidence.

Intellectual Growth Exercise: Engage in activities that stimulate intellectual growth. This could be reading the top 100 books or attending seminars or watching online information that adds to what you already know. Seek out a group of people who enjoy discussing topics for intellectual advancement.

Eric, a sharp-minded copy editor and manager of a cozy coffee shop, believes intellectual growth is as essential as caffeine in one's daily routine. Between editing projects and running a popular cafe, he attends online seminars focused on emerging trends in linguistics and effective communication. He also hosts a weekly "Books & Brews" evening at his shop, where he and others dive into discussions about classic literature, recent discoveries, and insightful podcasts.

Eric's gatherings spark new ideas for all who attend and welcome new 'thinkers' into the vibrant community of his coffee shop.

Deep Thinking Practice: Dedicate some quiet time for deep thinking. This could be thinking about a complex problem, planning, or reflecting on current topics of the day. If this is a new exercise for you, begin with a timer and set it for five minutes.

Sophia, a philosophy student, incorporates this into her daily morning routine. She finds that this practice both grounds her for the upcoming day and helps in her ability to recall material afterward.

Learn and Share: Take something you've studied deeply and find a way to share that knowledge in a meaningful, accessible format to a broader audience.

Brenda has spent years learning about sharks. What began as a personal interest evolved into extensive research, thoughtful analysis, and rare film footage collected through her travels and dives. Recently, she began planning a YouTube channel to bring this material to a wider audience.

For Brenda, it's not just about sharing facts—it's about helping others understand a misunderstood species, sparking curiosity, and creating a place for respectful, informed conversation.

Brenda's Conceptualizer strength lies not just in gathering knowledge, but in her thoughtful and creative approach to offering that knowledge to a broader community.

ADVANCED TIPS FOR PLAYING THE CONCEPTUALIZER ROLE

Whether the Conceptualizer Role ranks first or seventh in your unique role order, this section can help you rank up. Written in a Conceptualizer style with detailed, research-backed insights, it allows you to *practice* the role while you *learn* it.

First, we'll explore **curiosity**—the neurological and cognitive engine behind Conceptualizer thinking. You'll discover how curiosity fuels learning and memory, backed by neuroscience, along with practical strategies to cultivate an inquiring mindset—one that values *questions over answers* and fosters intellectual growth.

Next, we'll refine the **art of questioning**, a core skill for deep thinkers. Thoughtful questions don't just uncover information; they open doors to new perspectives and solutions. This section provides both simple and advanced questioning strategies, including techniques from philosophy, psychology, and business analysis to help you think, analyze, and solve more effectively.

Mastering the Conceptualizer Role means fostering curiosity, formulating insightful questions, and developing a system for acquiring and applying knowledge. Let's start with curiosity and why it is foundational for this role.

Curiouser and Curiouser

Curiosity—the drive to explore and understand—is the fuel of the Conceptualizer Role. It's more than just an intellectual habit; it's a *biological mechanism* hardwired into our brains.

Dr. Matthias Gruber and his team at the University of California, Davis, uncovered how curiosity not only engages the brain's reward circuits but activates the ventral striatum, a key area for motivation and learning. Their research revealed that when we are deeply curious, learning itself becomes pleasurable—our brains treat acquiring new knowledge like a rewarding experience.

Beyond motivation, curiosity enhances memory. The same study showed that information learned during heightened curiosity is more likely to be retained, even unrelated facts presented at the same time. This means curiosity primes the brain for learning, making it a crucial tool for anyone looking to deepen their understanding and recall complex information. But how do you intentionally cultivate curiosity?

The answer lies in developing a mindset that *values questions over answers*.

- Challenge your own assumptions—be willing to question long-held beliefs.

- Seek out opposing viewpoints—listen to perspectives that differ from your own.
- Engage with unfamiliar topics—intellectual stagnation occurs when we stay in our comfort zone.

Stanford psychologist Carol Dweck's research on "growth mindset" highlights how embracing the idea that intelligence and abilities *can* develop leads to greater resilience and curiosity. People with a fixed mindset avoid uncertainty, while those with a growth mindset thrive on it.

"I would rather have questions that can't be answered than answers that can't be questioned."—Richard Feynman

---

Like a muscle, curiosity strengthens with use. The Conceptualizer Role *requires* curiosity—it's the motivating force behind deeper thinking, sharper analysis, and better problem-solving.

The Art of Questioning

Just as curiosity fuels learning, questioning directs it. Strong questions challenge assumptions, uncover new insights, and refine understanding. They aren't just tools for gathering information—they are the keys to deeper thinking and better problem-solving. But asking the right question at the right time is a skill in itself.

Let's explore three powerful questioning techniques that will sharpen your ability to analyze, probe, and uncover meaningful answers.

Ask Open-Ended Questions

Open-ended questions are those that cannot be answered with a simple "yes" or "no." They invite exploration and promote deeper thought.

Ask questions that begin with the 5 Ws and H: who, what, when, where, why and how.

- "Who all is coming to the wedding?"
- "What has been done on the project so far?"
- "When did the problem start?"
- "Where should we be looking?"
- "Why is this done this way"
- "How does that relate to...?"

This simple yet powerful method is the go-to strategy for general information gathering. But when solving complex problems, deeper techniques are needed.

"Questions are places in your mind where answers fit. If you haven't asked the question, the answer has nowhere to go."
-Clayton Christensen

The Five Whys Method

This powerful technique, developed by Sakichi Toyoda, the founder of Toyota, is referred to as the Five Whys. When faced with a problem or issue, ask "why" five times to uncover the root cause. This method promotes a deeper understanding of the underlying factors involved.

- **Why are there so many defective widgets?** The machine is overheating.
- **Why is the machine overheating?** The cooling system is not effective.
- **Why is the cooling system not effective?** The cooling system's filter is clogged.

- **Why is the filter clogged?** It hasn't been replaced according to the maintenance schedule.
- **Why hasn't it been replaced on schedule?** The maintenance schedule is not properly monitored or enforced, indicating a need for better oversight and adherence to maintenance protocols.

This works for personal questions as well. For example, imagine you want to change a behavior or learn something new in your life and you are not seeing progress. The Five Whys can help to uncover the real cause for being demotivated.

- **Why don't I want to change or learn something new?** It feels overwhelming and requires effort.
- **Why does it feel overwhelming?** I'm unsure where to start or fear failing.
- **Why am I afraid of failing?** Failure might expose my vulnerabilities or incompetence.
- **Why does exposing vulnerabilities concern me?** It could lead to judgment or embarrassment.
- **Why am I worried about judgment?** I value others' opinions highly, possibly more than my own growth.

The answers to the Five Whys offers a method to trace the cause or root of an identified problem. Instead of accepting surface-level frustrations, you push yourself toward real solutions.

But what if your goal is to truly learn—gaining clarity and deepening your understanding? This requires more than just gathering information; it demands engaging with the material or situation in a meaningful way. In this case, the next technique is especially effective.

Think Like Socrates

Named after Socrates, the Socratic Method challenges assumptions and forces deeper thinking. It's used in law, philosophy, and critical analysis to refine reasoning.

Here's how it works. Ask yourself questions using this framework:

- **Clarification:** "What do I actually believe about this?"
- **Assumptions:** "What am I assuming is true?"
- **Rationale:** "What facts support my belief?"
- **Perspectives:** "How might someone else see this differently?"
- **Implications:** "What are the consequences of this idea?"

This method doesn't just deepen understanding—it promotes thinking, actually considering the impact of the questions you are asking. Let's look at an example around considering a job change. Here are some possible questions for each of the five areas:

- **Clarification:** "Why am I thinking about leaving my job?"
- **Assumptions:** "Am I assuming a new job will be better?"
- **Rationale:** "What evidence do I have that a change would improve my situation?"
- **Perspectives:** "How do others see my skills? What am I overlooking?"
- **Implications:** "What happens if I switch jobs and regret it? What happens if I don't switch jobs?"

This structured thinking prevents or at least slows down, impulsive decisions and helps promote better informed choices.

"It is the mark of an educated mind to be able to entertain a thought without accepting it."—Aristotle

---

Questioning the Question

Perhaps the most challenging yet insightful part of this process is stepping back to reflect on your own line of questioning. This is where true learning happens—not just in finding answers but in evaluating how the questions themselves shaped your understanding. Ask yourself:

- "Why did I ask these specific questions?"
- "What have I actually learned from this process?"
- "Did I ask the right questions, or was there a better approach?"

Engaging in *Questioning the Question* refines your ability to ask sharper, more effective questions in the future. It's a way of ensuring that your inquiry leads to meaningful insights rather than just reinforcing assumptions.

"Did you ask a good question today?" -Isaac Rabi

Great Questions

So, whether you're analyzing a complex problem, making a critical decision, or simply trying to understand the world around you, the Conceptualizer Role is there to help. When used well, it transforms confusion into clarity, questions into insights, and ideas into meaningful action.

The goal of the Conceptualizer Role is to ask the questions that acquire useful, factual, and comprehensive information. The Conceptualizer seeks to be an expert and it all begins with great questions.

Thinking Thoroughly

In the realm of thought, a Conceptualizer dwells,
A seeker of patterns in data's deep wells.
With an inquisitive mind that dissects and explores,
Unraveling mysteries, opening doors.

"Question everything," was Einstein's refrain,
The Conceptualizer agrees, again and again.
Question they must, for in doubt lies the key,
Unlocks the chains of thought, and sets the mind free.

They ponder, they probe, with logic so clear,
Turning chaos to order when solutions appear.
To deepen their craft, they tirelessly train,
Seeking the summit where true experts reign.

They wander through theories both new and arcane,
Finding strange beauty in logic's domain.
In silence they flourish, in stillness they grow,
Letting curiosity set the tempo.

Soaring on wings of relentless inquiry,
They craft their own legacy of intellect's tapestry.
In the realm of ideas, their dominion's profound,
With each answered query, new puzzles abound.

SUMMARY

This chapter explored the details of the Conceptualizer Role, highlighting its essential function as the bridge between knowledge and application. The Conceptualizer is more than just a thinker—it is the role of curiosity, logic, and discovery, continuously seeking to understand and explain the world.

🟡 How often do you ask "why" or "what if"?

We began with the story of Jer, illustrating the challenges that arise when this role is underutilized. Through his journey, we saw how adopting the Conceptualizer Role transforms uncertainty into clarity, strengthening both personal expertise and team success.

🟡 When was the last time you paused to analyze a situation before acting?

From there, we examined how the Conceptualizer Role fuels growth in both personal and professional settings—through logical reasoning, incisive questioning, and a relentless pursuit of understanding. Those who embrace this role are not just problem-solvers but insight-builders, helping others navigate complexity with greater ease.

🟡 Do you challenge assumptions, or do you accept things at face value?

A brief bulleted definition was included, followed by a comprehensive description of the Conceptualizer Role. Exercises were offered to help you practice this role, sharpening your ability to analyze, connect, and apply knowledge effectively.

The chapter then moved into advanced strategies, including promoting curiosity and several techniques for asking great questions.

🟡 What's one question you could ask today that might lead to a deeper insight?

Ultimately, this chapter serves as a roadmap for mastering the Conceptualizer Role. By developing this mindset, you position yourself as a lifelong learner, a skilled questioner, and a guide for others seeking clarity. But acquiring knowledge isn't the end goal—it's how you apply it that matters.

🟡 How will you use what you've learned from this chapter?

A strong Conceptualizer doesn't just accumulate knowledge—they make sense of it, challenge it, and share it in ways that deepen understanding and inspire mastery in others.

ONE QUICK TIP

Asking insightful, thought-provoking questions is a huge part of playing this role.

Questions not only spark curiosity and deepen understanding, but also stimulate innovative thinking and promote productive learning. Here are some sample Conceptualizer Role types of questions you can practice with:

- "What are the options?"
- "What information am I missing that could help me better understand?"
- "Have I shared what I have learned?"
- "What assumptions am I making, and are they valid?"
- "What patterns are in this data?"
- "How can I apply the lessons learned from the past to this current situation?"
- "Have I asked good questions today?"

Remember, the goal of asking these questions isn't necessarily to find immediate answers, but rather to think, learn, and understand more.

THOUGHTS FROM A CONCEPTUALIZER

I wanted to share some thoughts with you about the role I most often find myself playing in life, that of the Conceptualizer. Why, you might ask. The answer, quite simply, is the joy of discovery.

In my own journey, my mind is always in a state of active curiosity. I am constantly asking questions, only a fraction of which actually get verbalized. I am constantly seeking to understand more and better.

This curiosity is not a burden, but rather, it's a source of unending fascination. Every question I pose, every answer I unearth, is like untying a knot in the vast tapestry of knowledge. It's a process that fills me with a sense of wonderment, and it's one of the things I love most about being a Conceptualizer.

In terms of its usefulness, the Conceptualizer Role allows me to view the world from a multi-dimensional perspective. It's like possessing a mental compass that enables me to navigate through complexities and uncertainties. This doesn't mean I have all the answers; on the contrary, it means I try to find the right questions. And often, it's the questions that lead to the most enlightening answers.

Moreover, playing the Conceptualizer Role has taught me the value of deep and critical thinking, and the importance of evidence-based reasoning. I've learned to challenge assumptions, to push the boundaries of conclusions, and to continually seek patterns amidst the chaos. In doing so, I feel I've become a more thoughtful individual, definitely a better problem solver, and a more effective communicator.

There's a quote I often find myself coming back to, one that I think encapsulates the essence of being a Conceptualizer. It's by Albert Einstein, who said, "The important thing is not to stop questioning. Curiosity has its own reason for existing." It's this sentiment that inspires me to embrace the unknown, to question, to explore, and to learn.

Using the Conceptualizer Role isn't always easy, but the rewards it offers are truly fulfilling. If there's one thing I've learned from my journey so far, it's that there's always more to discover, more to understand, and more to appreciate.

Thank you for taking the time to read my thoughts. I hope they offer you a glimpse into the joy and value I find in the Conceptualize Role. Perhaps they might even inspire you to explore this role for yourself.

UNIT IV: PUTTING THE ROLES TO WORK FOR YOU
FOR THE ROLE MASTERS

THIS MAY BE the most practical—and potentially the most transformative—section of this entire book. The roles show you what you can do. Pairing them shows you how to do it better. It's where individual strengths evolve into a flexible, real-world toolkit you can use again and again.

But first, a note of caution. This section won't make much sense if you don't have a general understanding of all Seven Roles.

If you've done the work in the earlier chapters, you're ready. You know the language. You've seen the roles in action.

If you're not quite there yet, no problem. Take a moment to revisit the earlier chapters. This section will still be here when you're ready and you'll get more from it when you come back.

But if you *are* ready—if you're curious about how roles work together, how they shift, and how to use that to build a deeper understanding in yourself and your relationships—then let's begin.

Onward for the Seven Roles!

ROLE PAIRING
MIXING AND MATCHING THE ROLES

THE DANCE of Roles

Imagine role pairing like a dance. In any good dance, one partner leads while the other follows—but both are moving to the same rhythm, each adding something essential to the performance. In the same way, role pairing brings together two complementary roles: one typically leads, setting the tone or approach, while the other follows, enhancing and supporting the outcome.

Why does this dance of roles matter? Because in real life, we rarely play just one role all the time. In one situation, we might lean into the Conceptualizer Role—curious, analytical, and eager to understand how things work. But in the next moment, we might switch to the Luminary Role—energizing others, sharing big ideas, and creating excitement. When we pair these roles intentionally, we become more adaptable, more creative, and more effective.

And just like dancers can switch who's leading, the lead role in a pairing can shift based on the moment. A Conceptualizer/Luminary leads with analysis and insight, while a Luminary/Conceptualizer leads with energy and presence. That leading role influences not just what gets done, but *how* it gets done.

Let's look at an example. Lila and Rake are newly married and shopping for their first car. They both bring strong perspectives to the table. Lila is a Luminary/Conceptualizer (LC)—full of energy and vision. She imagines a car that reflects their adventurous spirit and turns heads in the parking lot. Her enthusiasm is contagious, and her favorite flashy models come with detailed stories about the life they'll live in them.

Rake, a Conceptualizer/Luminary (CL), starts from a different place. He's focused on reliability, fuel efficiency, and long-term value. He's done his homework, complete with spreadsheets and safety ratings, and while he also wants a great-looking car, his version of "wow" includes function as much as form.

Together, their roles don't compete—they complement. Lila keeps the experience joyful and bold; Rake keeps it grounded and intentional. Their role pairing leads to a richer outcome than either could create alone. That's the power of knowing your roles and using them in harmony.

Together, their differing perspectives create a balanced approach to car shopping. Lila's excitement makes the car shopping experience enjoyable, while Rake's analytical insights keep their search focused and practical. Both want a standout car, but their definitions of 'wow' differ. As they navigate the decision-making process, they demonstrate how effective role pairing can promote collaborative wow results.

ROLE MASTERY

Role pairing isn't just a helpful strategy—it's a key part of the journey toward 'role mastery'.

To truly master the Seven Roles means more than knowing what each role is or does. It's requires understanding how each one thinks, behaves, and influences the world. It's learning to move fluidly between roles—not out of habit or pressure, but with practiced ease and purpose.

The first step is simply noticing. Pay attention to how you already shift roles throughout your day. You might find yourself in the Organizer Role at work, structuring timelines and managing moving parts, and then naturally shift into the Team Builder Role at home, making sure family plans include everyone's preferences. These shifts often happen without conscious thought—but bringing awareness to them is the first sign that mastery is beginning.

From there, self reflection is key. Ask yourself why you're choosing certain roles in different situations. You might reach for the Prophet Role during a brainstorming session at work, wanting to introduce fresh ideas. Then, in a more personal moment, you find yourself in the Implementor Role—volunteering your time and energy because you want to make a difference in a tangible way. Understanding your motivation adds a layer of intentionality to your actions and reveals the deeper values behind your choices.

As you continue observing your roles, it becomes important to notice their impact. The roles you use don't just shape your outcomes—they shape how others experience you. Bringing the Luminary Role into a business meeting might energize the team, just as using that same role among friends can foster connection and a sense of shared enthusiasm. Seeing how your roles affect others helps you grow into them more fully and more flexibly.

With this insight, you can begin to choose roles more strategically. You might use the Investor Role in your career to identify long-term partnerships or promising ventures. Then, later that evening, step into the Organizer Role at home to bring calm and structure to a chaotic moment. The more aligned your role choice is with your goals, the more effective—and impactful—you become.

This is where role pairing begins to unlock new potential. Combining roles expands your capacity. Practicing pairs allows you to see how the strengths of one role support the strengths of another. When you move between the Luminary and Implementor Roles, for example, you're not just inspiring others with enthusiasm—you're also making sure things actually get done. That pairing turns bright ideas into real progress.

Or consider the Prophet and Investor Roles. Paired together, they offer vision and discernment. The Prophet imagines what's possible; the Investor asks if it's worth pursuing. Together, they help you choose opportunities that are both meaningful and sustainable. You can dream big and stay grounded at the same time.

Ultimately, Role Mastery is about flexibility. It's not about using all seven roles equally—it's about knowing them well enough to shift your mindset and actions as needed. Mastery is choosing the right role for the right moment, paired in the right combination. And that ability to pair roles wisely and fluidly is what turns knowledge into growth, and growth into impact.

ROLE BURNOUT

Balancing role mastery with an awareness of *role burnout* is essential. Burnout doesn't always come from doing too much—it can also come from playing too much of the same role. When we overuse a particular role, even one we excel at, we risk draining our energy and our enthusiasm. Likewise, when we're forced into roles that don't feel natural or are especially difficult to maintain, we can experience exhaustion more quickly. Over time, a role imbalance can dull our effectiveness and leave us feeling disconnected from both the task and the people around us.

Role pairing can be a powerful protector for role burnout. Instead of relying on a single role to carry the weight, pairing roles allows us to shift our mindset, distribute our energy differently, and bring fresh perspective to familiar situations. For example, if you often find yourself in the Organizer Role—focused on planning, systems, and control—it may begin to feel like everything depends on you. But intentionally bringing in the Team Builder Role can soften that burden. A more collaborative approach creates community support, relieves pressure, and might even bring joy back in through connection with others.

Sometimes burnout also reveals what's missing. When something feels off, it's often because we're either overplaying a role or avoiding one that could help. Reflecting on what isn't working—whether it's frustration, boredom, or resistance—can point you toward a role that might restore balance. The solution isn't always to push harder in the same direction. It might be to shift roles entirely.

When you engage in role pairing, you create a more sustainable rhythm. You gain the ability to pivot when needed, to see problems from more than one angle, and to lead with more resilience. This flexibility not only guards against burnout—it deepens your skill and confidence across all Seven Roles.

In the next section, we'll explore how to bring role pairing into your daily rhythm so it becomes second nature—a powerful tool for both avoiding burnout and expanding your capacity.

INTERNAL ROLE PAIRING: MASTERING YOUR OWN DANCE

We all use multiple roles all the time. Sometimes we're in the Prophet Role, other times the Conceptualizer Role. We should be open to shifting to the Organizer, Implementor, Luminary, Team Builder, or Investor Role as circumstances require.

Internal role pairing requires an understanding of ourselves and how we play each the roles. as well as the ways in which we combine them. these different aspects of ourselves and learning how to combine them and transition between them effectively.

To start mastering your own dance, you first need to identify your prominent roles. Ask yourself, which roles do you naturally gravitate towards? Maybe you're a keen Conceptualizer, always eager to dive deep into a problem and find out more. Or perhaps you're more of a Prophet, always looking forward with new ideas, anticipating what's next and seeking change.

Once you've identified your dominant roles, think about which one often takes the lead and which one follows. Is there a pattern? Do you tend to start as a Conceptualizer and then shift into the Prophet Role once you have a clear understanding of the problem? Or is it the other way around? Or do you avoid some roles altogether?

Being aware of your role dynamics can help you adapt your approach depending on the situation. For example, if you're faced with a complex challenge, you might decide to lead with the Conceptualizer Role to analyze the situation thoroughly. But if the challenge calls for immediate action, you might lead with the Prophet Role or maybe even the Luminary Role to quickly engage and move forward.

However, remember that the goal is not to rigidly sticking to one role or another. Just like a good dancer, you need to be flexible and ready to switch roles when the rhythm of the situation changes.

Mastering this internal dance with each of the Seven Roles can help you become more versatile, adaptable, and effective in various contexts.

Examples of Role Pairing

To put this into practice, let's look at an example. Suppose you're a business owner and your dominant roles are Investor and Implementor. When a new investment opportunity comes your way, you might initially lead with the Investor Role, evaluating the potential returns and risks. Once you've made a decision, you might switch to the Implementor Role to put the plan into action. This way, you're leveraging both roles effectively, allowing you to harness their strengths while minimizing their potential weaknesses.

However, as you continue to dance between these roles, you might find yourself feeling overwhelmed or stretched too thin. This could be a sign that you're neglecting other important roles, such as the Prophet Role, to know where you are going, or the Team Builder for nurturing relationships with your team. Or perhaps the project is too unmanageable and requires the Organizer Role to create a plan, or you don't have sufficient data to make a decision so require more of the Conceptualizer Role.

You can also pair roles in unique ways to tackle specific challenges. For example, combining the Team Builder's empathetic understanding with the Implementor's practical action can be incredibly powerful when dealing with conflicts or morale issues. Similarly, pairing the Prophet's forward-thinking perspective with the Investor's strategic decision-making can be highly effective in navigating change and uncertainty.

Remember, mastering your internal role pairing dance isn't about rigidly defining or restricting yourself to certain roles. It's about understanding your strengths and tendencies, being adaptable and flexible, and strategically leveraging different aspects of yourself to navigate various situations effectively. It's an ongoing journey of self-discovery and role growth that can significantly enhance your effectiveness and your fulfillment.

Here are a few more specific examples of internal role pairing to help reach goals.

Moving Homes: Let's say you are moving homes. The Prophet Role steps in to decide to make the move. The Conceptualizer Role helps you clarify the options available where you are moving, helping to determine the best possible location. The Investor Role maximizes value. The Luminary Role imagines the activities and people flow. The Organizer Role helps in planning and preparing for the move. When it's time to actually move, the Implementor takes over, executing the plan and making sure everything goes smoothly. And unless you plan to move solo, it is best to keep the Team Builder Role on call.

Planning a Vacation: Planning a vacation requires different roles. You need the Prophet Role to envision the perfect holiday, the Conceptualizer Role to research and understand the logistics, and the Organizer to plan the itinerary. Finally, the Luminary keeps the excitement going and ensures you make the most of your vacation.

Pursuing a New Hobby: The Luminary within you ignites interest in a new hobby, say gardening. The Prophet enables you to envision a beautiful garden at your home. The Conceptualizer helps you research about different plants, and the Implementor helps you put it all into action.

Managing Personal Finances: The Investor takes the lead in managing your personal finances, keeping track of expenses and making investment decisions. However, the Prophet might come into play to envision long-term financial goals, and the Organizer will help in setting up a system to manage day-to-day finances.

Fitness Goals: The Prophet Role helps you envision your future self in better shape. The Luminary Role motivates you to start a new workout regimen. The Conceptualizer Role learns about different workout methods and diet plans, and the Implementor Role ensures you follow through.

Launching a New Project: At the beginning of a new project, the Prophet Role will help you envision the project's outcome and the Investor Role will evaluate the project's potential return on investment. The Conceptualizer Role will research and design the project, and the Implementor will execute it.

Leading a Team: As a team leader, the Team Builder helps you foster a positive and cooperative work environment. The Conceptualizer offers expertise, while the Organizer ensures everything runs smoothly.

Managing a Crisis: In a crisis, the Prophet Role helps envision a path out of the crisis. The Conceptualizer Role enables you to understand the situation and come up with potential solutions. The Implementor then executes the plan, and the Luminary keeps the morale up.

Building a Startup: In building a startup, you likely need to play all the roles. The Prophet Role helps you envision the startup's future, the Conceptualizer designs the product or service, the Investor secures funding, and the Implementor gets things done. The Team Builder fosters a positive culture and motivates the team and the Organizer keeps it all running efficiently.

Remember, there's no one-size-fits-all approach in role pairing. It's a personal dance, unique to you and your rhythm. The key is to be mindful of your roleset and their interplay, and to consciously decide which one leads and which one follows depending on the circumstances.

EXTERNAL ROLE PLAY OR HOW TO DANCE WITH OTHERS

Just as role pairing can happen within us, it can also happen between us. External role pairing means noticing how your roles interact with the others roles—it's a shared choreography, where each person brings their own rhythm, mindset, and movement.

In the dance of life, we rarely move alone. Every day we engage with people whose roles may complement or contrast with our own. Understanding the roles others are playing can transform how we communicate, collaborate, and connect. It allows us to approach relationships with insight and flexibility that can minimize or prevent frustration or confusion.

To master this external dance, begin by observing. Ask yourself: Does this person tend to organize details and keep things on track? Do they light up a room with energy and new ideas? Are they focused on harmony, or always pushing for a better future? These simple observations can offer clues to someone's dominant roles. If you're unsure, there's a brief quiz in the appendix to help you identify the roles others may naturally lean into.

Once you have a sense of their role, ask yourself how it relates to yours. Do their strengths balance your gaps? Do they bring something you don't—or do they double down on your tendencies, for better or worse? Knowing this can help you adjust your expectations and communication style. If their role complements yours, you might partner with ease. If it clashes, you may need to step back, reframe, and find common ground.

For example, imagine you're a Team Builder, collaborating with a Conceptualizer on a project. While the Conceptualizer excels at analyzing the problem and crafting a smart solution, they may struggle to keep the group aligned and cooperative. Your ability to foster collaboration fills in that gap. Together, the two of you can cover both the *what* and the *how* of success.

But sometimes pairing happens with someone who shares your role—say, a Conceptualizer working with another Conceptualizer. While the ideas may flow freely, conflict can arise over who owns the vision or whose approach is more precise. In those moments, it helps to agree on structure ahead of time—who leads, who supports, and how each voice will be heard.

External pairing isn't limited to one-on-one relationships. Consider your audience during a presentation: are they expecting the bold vision of a Prophet, the enthusiasm of a Luminary, the clarity of a Conceptualizer, or the encouragement of a Team Builder? Knowing what roles your listeners value can shape how you prepare, how you speak, and how your message lands.

Ultimately, external role pairing is more than simply working well with others. It's about co-creating something better than you could alone. It requires effort, empathy, and the maturity to see not just your own strengths but the strengths in those around you.

Mastery at this level means knowing your own roles, recognizing what you need, and welcoming the unique ways others can meet you there. It's not requiring that you change who you are—or expecting others to change for you. It's finding the rhythm between roles and dancing with it.

Beyond You...Mastering Roles Together

Mastering external role pairing isn't easy. It requires effort, patience, open communication, and mature self-awareness. But when done well, it leads to more productive collaborations and deeper, more meaningful relationships.

The dance with others isn't about changing who you are or forcing others to change. It's recognizing each person's unique approach and adopting the best mindset and communication style to create the desired impact.

External role pairing takes the most effort—first because you need to understand your own role strengths, then you need to recognize what you are missing and finally, and  most challenging, you need to find that role in others. This is the highest level of role mastery: seeing the strengths in others, aligning them with your own, and working together to accomplish more than would be possible apart.

PUTTING IT ALL TOGETHER: EXAMPLES AND APPLICATION

Now that you understand both internal and external role pairing, let's look at how they come to life in everyday situations. The following examples illustrate how recognizing and applying roles—within yourself and in your relationships—can lead to more clarity, impact, and ultimately, better connections.

Example 1 – Personal Growth

Imagine you strongly play the **Luminary/Implementor** roles. You're great at inspiring others with your enthusiasm and vision, and you excel at executing plans and getting things done. However, when it comes to financial decisions, you might struggle—perhaps jumping in too quickly, driven by excitement rather than carefully assessing the long-term viability of an investment. Maybe you've had moments where a bold idea seemed like a sure win—until the numbers didn't add up, or an overlooked detail created unexpected risk.

Now, you have two options. You could strengthen your Investor Role internally by deliberately learning more about finance—taking courses, reading books, or seeking mentorship to build a more strategic mindset around investments. This might not come naturally at first, but developing even a basic financial framework could help you make more informed decisions.

Alternatively, you could pair up externally with someone who plays the Investor Role exceptionally well. Picture a business partner, mentor, or trusted advisor who thrives on analyzing risks, weighing long-term potential, and making data-driven choices. This person wouldn't stifle your enthusiasm—they would refine and focus it, helping you channel your passion into investments and decisions that are both exciting and sustainable. With their insight balancing your drive, you can keep doing what you do best—generating ideas, inspiring action, and getting things done—while knowing that the financial side is in capable hands.

This is the power of role mastery—knowing when to develop a role within yourself and when to lean on the strengths of others.

Example 2 – Project Management

Suppose you are leading a high-stakes project at work. You're comfortable in the **Organizer/Implementor** roles—you quickly grasp the core problem, break it down into manageable parts, and meticulously plan out solutions. You're detail-oriented, organized, and methodical in execution—but despite all that structure, team dynamics feel off. Meetings seem disjointed, some team members are disengaged, and others are frustrated because they don't feel heard.

You might assume that everyone is as motivated by the plan as you are, but in reality, different personalities require different levels and styles of engagement. Some need encouragement, some need clarity, and some just need to know their voice matters.

Now, you have two options. You could strengthen your Team Builder Role internally by making a conscious effort to engage with your team —actively listening to concerns, ensuring everyone has a role that plays to their strengths, and fostering an environment where collaboration thrives. You might set aside time in meetings for open discussion, give recognition more intentionally, or use feedback to adjust your leadership style.

Alternatively, you could pair externally by inviting someone strong in the Team Builder Role to co-lead the project. Picture a colleague who naturally fosters team spirit, understands group dynamics, and ensures that every voice is heard. They thrive on motivation, morale, and making sure people feel valued. By having them focus on maintaining team harmony, you can stay in your zone of genius—refining strategies, structuring solutions, and ensuring the execution stays on track.

This is the power of role mastery—knowing when to develop a role within yourself and when to lean on others to create the strongest possible outcome.

Example 3 – Parent-Child Relationship

Let's say you naturally lean toward the **Prophet/Conceptualizer** roles —you're skilled at anticipating future trends, analyzing complex systems, and thinking several steps ahead. You encourage your child to consider the bigger picture, make thoughtful decisions, and prepare for what's coming. However, your child is wired differently. They thrive in the **Implementor/Luminary** roles, bringing energy, action, and a hands-on approach to everything they do. They are focused on execution, prefer learning by doing, and love engaging with others in a charismatic, present-moment way.

These differences can sometimes lead to disconnects. You might try to explain why something matters, while your child just wants to know what needs to be done right now. You may get frustrated when they seem uninterested in long-term goals, while they may feel overwhelmed or uninspired by your seemingly abstract ideas.

Understanding these role differences can transform the way you engage with your child. Instead of explaining a concept in theoretical terms, you might demonstrate it through action, giving them a hands-on way to experience the idea. If you want to encourage better decision-making, instead of talking through scenarios in depth, you could make it interactive—letting them test and adjust as they go. Adding enthusiasm and tangible examples will make your message resonate more with their Implementor and Luminary strengths.

At the same time, recognizing and nurturing their natural talents allows you to support their growth in a meaningful way. You might encourage their Implementor skills by giving them practical projects where they can take the lead—such as helping with a home improvement task, organizing an event, or managing a responsibility within the family. Their Luminary skills could be developed through team activities, leadership roles in school, or public speaking opportunities, helping them use their natural charisma in positive and constructive ways.

By adapting your approach and meeting them where they are, you're not only strengthening your connection but also empowering them to grow into their strengths while appreciating yours. This is the essence of role awareness in parenting—balancing guidance with adaptability to promote growth. When you adjust your style to connect with their roles, you model flexibility and invite cooperation—not just compliance.

Example 4 – Romantic Relationships or Dating

Let's say you're someone who naturally plays the **Luminary/Team Builder** roles in a dating relationship. You bring energy, fun, and genuine care—you're always planning experiences, sharing ideas, and trying to make your partner feel connected and supported. Your joy often sets the tone for shared time together. But when conflict arises or difficult conversations need to happen, you may find yourself hesitant to address them directly, preferring to keep things light and harmonious.

Your partner, on the other hand, leads with the **Prophet/Organizer** roles. They value clarity, purpose, and structure. They're not afraid to challenge the status quo or bring up tough topics if it means creating a more honest, future-focused relationship. While this can feel intense at times, it also brings depth, direction, and intentionality to your connection.

If you're not aware of these differences, it's easy to misunderstand each other—your partner may feel you're avoiding important issues, while you may feel they're being too serious or critical. But understanding your roles makes room for a better rhythm. When you recognize that your Luminary/Team Builder strengths bring joy and warmth, and their Prophet/Organizer strengths bring vision and clarity, you can begin to play off each other more consciously.

You might stretch yourself by stepping into a more grounded role—drawing from the Conceptualizer to reflect before reacting, or the Organizer to bring calm structure to your thoughts. Meanwhile, your partner might lean into the Team Builder Role to ensure their concerns are shared in a way that invites collaboration rather than conflict.

In romantic partnerships, as in all relationships, role awareness creates room for empathy, growth, and deeper connection. It allows you to see differences not as friction points, but as invitations to balance one another and move forward together.

"It is not our differences that divide us. It is our inability to recognize, accept, and celebrate those differences."
— *Audre Lorde*

In each of these situations—whether personal, professional, parental or relational—role pairing offers a practical path forward. It invites self-reflection, mutual understanding, and the kind of growth that happens when we play to strengths—ours and others'.

These examples show that role pairing isn't just a theoretical concept —it's a practical tool for navigating real life. Whether you're leading a project, raising a child, building a business, or growing a relationship, the ability to recognize and adjust your roles—internally and externally—can transform the way you engage with the world.

The more fluent you become in all Seven Roles, the more confidence you'll have to shift, stretch, and collaborate in ways that lead to better outcomes and deeper connection.

That's the heart of role mastery: knowing who you are, appreciating who others are, and choosing your roles with intention.

CONCLUSION

Role pairing is an amazing tool to both better understand ourselves and to interact with others.

The dance of roles isn't about changing who you are. It's about recognizing your rhythm, moving with intention, and choosing partners who help you grow. Some will move in sync with you. Others won't. Both teach you something.

A great relationship is about two things: first, appreciating the similarities, and second, respecting the differences. It's a dance, not a duel. In Team Builder language, it's about creating harmony in the dance of life— knowing when to lead, when to follow, and when to shift…roles.

"A great relationship is about two things: first, appreciating the similarities, and second, respecting the differences. It's a dance, not a duel."

UNIT V: THE END OR IS IT THE BEGINNING?

ONWARD!

As we reach the end of this book, it's both an end and a beginning. It's the end of a journey of learning the Seven Roles. But now the real adventure begins—the one where you apply what you've discovered.

You now have seven tools to choose from. Some may feel natural. Others might need practice. But every role is yours to choose. When you need direction, step into the Prophet Role. When things feel scattered, turn to the Organizer. To inspire others—or yourself—call on the Luminary. To move something forward, use the Implementor. To build trust, bring in the Team Builder. When it's time to plan for growth, think like an Investor. And when you need to slow down and make sense of things, the Conceptualizer is ready.

You don't have to be everything. You just have to be someone who's willing to start, open to change, and brave enough to play the role that moves you forward. The roles offer insight, you provide the action.

My hope is that the Seven Roles help you meet your goals with courage, lead your most important relationships with love, and live out your biggest, most outrageous, life dreams with purpose.

Be more..you.

. . .

"You never change your life until you step out of your comfort zone; change begins at the end of your comfort zone." -Roy T. Bennett

Thank you for reading this book. Team Builder comments and Conceptualizer questions are always welcome!
Send to SevenRoles@gmail.com or visit us at SevenRoles.com.

QUICK QUIZ
YOU GET AN "A"

This quiz is intended to help you determine your role strengths and weaknesses. A few questions are included for each role to help you assess how well you play it.

Remember to think about how well or how often you play each of the roles and in what environments. For example, you might focus on using the Organizer Role at work and the Implementor Role at home. Or consider how you might have played the Prophet Role in the past but now your focus is more on the Team Builder Role.

Roles are fluid. The whole idea of this book is to figure out how and when you play each role and how and when you should change roles to better meet your goals.

Here are the questions that are included in each chapter to help you assess your role strengths--and weaknesses.

Prophet Role

- Do you think creatively and see things from a unique, new or different perspective?

- Are you comfortable in chaotic situations and do you adapt to change quickly?
- Are you willing to take risks and withstand criticism in pursuit of your vision?
- Do your ideas challenge the status quo?

Organizer Role

- Are you able to break down complex tasks into manageable steps?
- Do you focus on planning out your goals?
- Are you efficient in your work?
- Are you good at multitasking? Overseeing projects?

Luminary Role

- Are you engaging and inspiring to those around you?
- Do you have an enthusiastic outlook on life?
- Are you communicative and able to energize those around you?
- Do you know a lot of people and keep in touch?

Investor Role

- Are you strategic in your decision-making?
- Do you evaluate potential outcomes and risks before taking action?
- Are you inclusive and seek out diverse perspectives?
- Do you maintain a network of useful connections?

Team Builder Role

- Are you empathetic in your interactions?
- Do you value collaboration?
- Are you supportive of and trusted by others?

- Are you able to calm someone down?

Implementor Role

- Are you practical and task-focused?
- Do you take immediate action when you see something that needs to be done?
- Are you quick to volunteer your help?
- Do you get stuff done?!

Conceptualizer Role

- Are you data-focused in your decision-making?
- Do you seek out new knowledge and understanding of complex issues?
- Are you curious about the world around you?
- Do you share what you learn with others?

YOUR ROLE'DEX
A GLOSSARY OF KEY TERMS

This is a quick-reference guide to the Seven Roles—definitions and key terms, all in one place. The roles are easier to remember if you think of the word **POLITIC**. Each letter stands for one of the Seven Roles:

Prophet, **O**rganizer, **L**uminary, **I**mplementor, **T**eam Builder, **I**nvestor, and **C**onceptualizer.

Prophet Role: A visionary role thriving in change and chaos with out-of-the-box thinking. Operates within well-defined boundaries fueled by personal values. This role quickly analyzes and critiques ideas, predicting end results, and actively seeks innovative solutions.

Organizer Role: The Organizer brings order to chaos, excels at time management, enjoys working with established systems and processes, and advocates for detailed planning. They assess progress, optimize for efficiency, and work towards removing obstacles to streamline processes.

Luminary Role: Known for their communication skills, Luminaries inspire and motivate others. They build wide networks, enjoy being around people, and often find themselves in leadership roles. Luminaries are adaptable, spontaneous, and act as catalysts for change.

Investor Role: This role is financially savvy, profit-focused, skilled in negotiations, and values relationships. They prioritize sustainability over short-term gains and are proactive in securing resources and opportunities. This role is also characterized by generosity.

Team Builder Role: The Team Builder Role exhibits high emotional intelligence, manages relationships effectively, builds consensus, and promotes inclusiveness. This role actively listens to others, provides emotional support, and focuses on the team's collective goals.

Implementor Role: The Implementor takes a proactive approach to work, visualizes strategic steps, assists others, and showcases persistence. This role is detail-oriented, reliable, and practical, ensuring tasks are completed efficiently and thoroughly.

Conceptualizer Role: Conceptualizers are deep thinkers, investigative, data-driven, inquisitive, and experts in their field. They value accuracy, have a strong desire for continuous learning, and excel in pattern recognition and dissecting complex systems.

DEFINITIONS OF OTHER RELEVANT TERMS AND PHRASES

Role Play: The act of embodying a particular role or character, often with the purpose of understanding that role's perspectives, motivations, or behaviors better. In the context of the Seven Roles, Role play involves an individual consciously adopting the behaviors and mindset associated with a particular role to gain new perspectives or approaches to solve a specific problem.

Role Pairing: The combination of two roles, either within an individual or between two individuals, that work together to complement each other. The benefits of role pairing include a broader perspective, increased creativity, and the ability to handle a wider range of tasks or challenges.

Internal Role Pairing: This refers to an individual leveraging two or more of their roles to balance or enhance their approach to a task or challenge. For instance, an individual might use their Implementor Role to get things done while also drawing on their Conceptualizer Role to ensure they are considering all relevant factors and potential impacts.

External Role Pairing: This is when two individuals, each strong in different roles, work together to combine their strengths. This is a form of collaboration that can lead to increased effectiveness, creativity, and the ability to handle a broader range of tasks or challenges.

Role Flexibility: The ability to adapt and switch between different roles as the situation requires. Role flexibility allows an individual to respond effectively to various challenges, drawing on different strengths and approaches depending on what is most beneficial in the current context.

RoleSet: A term used to describe an individual's ordered list of the Seven Roles from strongest to weakest. A person's roleset provides insight into their natural tendencies and strengths, as well as areas where they may need to stretch or develop. Understanding one's roleset can aid in personal development, decision-making, daily interactions, work approach, and navigating relationships. Unlike fixed traits, a roleset is dynamic and can shift based on your focus, experience, and situational needs.

Role Mastery: Role Mastery involves a deep understanding of the Seven Roles, including behaviors, mindset, and approach. It includes recognizing these roles in your own actions, understanding why and how you use them, and seeing their impact on others or on goals. Additionally, it means identifying these roles in others, understanding their different approaches, and how each affects interactions.

Mastery involves an ongoing process of learning, practicing, and refining one's approach to each role, with the goal of becoming adept at recognizing and enacting the most appropriate role in a given situation.

Role Burnout: Role Burnout describes a state of exhaustion and diminished interest resulting from the excessive demand or overuse of a specific role, either due to external expectations or personal inclination towards familiar behaviors. This condition emerges when the continuous application of the same role depletes an individual's enthusiasm and effectiveness, leading to a reduction in their ability to perform the role. It underscores the importance of role diversity and the need for balance to maintain productivity.

STRS: STRS, or Seven Team Roles Scale, is a tool introduced in 2018 designed to assess the roles individuals naturally adopt within a team setting. It has undergone rigorous validation processes to ensure its reliability and accuracy. Since its release, it has been utilized by thousands of individuals, serving as a resource for understanding team dynamics and enhancing team performance.

"You never change things by fighting the existing reality. To change something, build a new model that makes the existing model obsolete."
-Buckminster Fuller

FOR THE CONCEPTUALIZER
THIS SECTION IS FOR THOSE WHO ALWAYS ASK: "BUT WHERE DID THIS COME FROM?"

Where Did the Seven Roles Come From?

People often ask where the Seven Roles came from. The short answer is: they've always been there—woven into how people contribute, connect, lead, support, and make meaning in the world. The longer answer is that I spent years observing patterns, testing possibilities, and eventually building a reliable, statistically valid way to measure what I had been seeing all along.

The Early Inspiration

The inspiration began in an unexpected place: Romans 12. This passage, often read in faith communities, describes seven "gifts"—distinct ways people successfully contribute to the whole. What struck me wasn't just the spiritual significance, but the practical clarity. These descriptions aligned with real-life behaviors and mindsets I had seen repeatedly in families, workplaces, and communities. What if these were more than theological categories? What if they pointed to enduring roles all people naturally play in team dynamics?

The goal became to see whether these ideas could be translated into something broader—something that would make sense to people regardless of background, belief system, or profession. So I began building a psychological framework based on the core idea that people have role-based ways of contributing, and that these roles could be observed, named, and eventually measured.

From Observation to Measurement

The early drafts of what would become the Seven Team Roles Scale (STRS) were grounded in over a decade of clinical, coaching, and consulting work. Consistent role patterns emerged in how people solved problems, communicated, delegated, and led. Those observations led to the first set of scale items—statements that reflected the thinking, behavior, and values of each role.

But more than pattern recognition was needed. I needed data.

A formal research study was begun using a large and diverse sample (N = 798), gathered primarily through Amazon Mechanical Turk, a well-established platform in academic research. Participants came from various professional, geographic, religious, and non-religious backgrounds. This broad reach offered a way to evaluate whether the structure of the Seven Roles would hold up across different worldviews.

Exploratory factor analysis (EFA) revealed that the items grouped naturally into the seven hypothesized roles. The factor structure aligned closely with the original conceptual model. Each role emerged as a distinct, statistically supported cluster of items:

- **Prophet** – vision-driven, values-oriented, boundary-setting
- **Organizer** – systems-focused, efficiency-seeking, process-minded
- **Luminary** – dynamic, relational, energizing
- **Implementor** – task-focused, steady, action-oriented
- **Team Builder** – empathetic, connecting, inclusive
- **Investor** – discerning, resource-aware, long-term thinking

- **Conceptualizer** – analytical, curious, pattern-seeking

Each role demonstrated internal consistency (Cronbach's alpha ≥ 0.70) and was statistically distinct from the others, confirming discriminant validity.

To establish convergent validity, the STRS was compared with the TwIVI scale, a well-established values-based measure grounded in Shalom Schwartz's theory of human values. The correlations were clear and compelling: each role aligned with specific values such as Benevolence, Achievement, Self-Direction, and Security.

This confirmed something that had already been observed in practice: the Seven Roles framework isn't just behavioral; it reflects the motivational forces that guide how people contribute. One of the most powerful insights from this process was recognizing that change doesn't begin with action—it begins with values. When people shift what they value, they naturally shift how they lead, connect, and grow. The Seven Roles give language to that shift.

Accessible to All Backgrounds

Although the original inspiration came from a spiritual source, the scale was intentionally written in nonreligious language. Importantly, there was no significant difference in how people from religious and nonreligious backgrounds responded to the items. The roles resonated broadly and accessibly across belief systems, confirming that the framework could be used in both faith-based and secular environments.

Practical Application

The final result was a psychometrically validated, easy-to-administer tool: the Seven Team Roles Scale, STRS. Since its release, it has been used by thousands of people across industries and continents—in corporations, schools, coaching sessions, leadership retreats, churches, small groups, and family settings.

Change begins with what we value. And from there, everything else shifts.

It helps individuals quickly identify their current 'roleset' or roles strengths. This could be to identify what roles they most naturally lead with, so they can maximize their strengths with greater confidence. Or it could be to identify what role they need to focus on to achieve a goal or purpose. As the roles become easier to identify they support stronger collaboration by offering insights into others rulesets. When people understand not only their own role but the roles of those around them, they communicate more clearly, resolve conflict more effectively, and build trust more quickly. In short: understanding roles enhances understanding of people.

Why It Matters

In the end, this scale wasn't about proving a theory—it was about giving people language for something many already feel: that we each have a way we most naturally contribute. And we're at our best not when we try to play every role at once, but when we lead with our strongest role and shift when the situation calls for something different.

That's what the Seven Roles offer: a framework for growth, connection, and clarity—grounded in observation, refined by data, and designed for real life. Your life.

"Go confidently in the direction of your dreams."—Henry David Thoreau

---

CREDITS

Photography: Epigraph Photo, and Author Photos by Kevan McConlogue, used with permission

Foreword: Family Photo (photographer unknown)

Individual Seven Roles Logos: AI-generated using DALL·E (by OpenAI), and further edited by Erin McConlogue

Google Event Photo: Screenshot taken from a video shared by Google

Seven Roles Logo: Designed by Quinlan Smith

Seven Roles Scale Screenshot: Taken from MyTeamRole.com

All Other Book Artwork: AI-assisted using DALL·E, with refinements and final edits in Canva by the author

Book Design Software: Vellum

Book Cover: Designed by 100Covers (100covers.com) Special shoutout to Jamie Ty who patiently handled the many revisions.

ACKNOWLEDGMENTS

This book—and the framework it presents—exists because of grace. I'm deeply grateful to God for the spark that began this journey and for the guidance all along the way.

Bringing the roles to life has been a 30-year journey, and I could not have reached this point without the support, insight, and encouragement of so many incredible people—especially my husband, **Sean**.

For 40 truly wonderful years, you've been the best part of every day, my steadfast supporter, and the first to take the Seven Team Roles Scale (because yes, it's always a race). Thank you for believing in me.

And Patrick, Kevan, Erin, and Meaghan—each of you, now incredible adults and true friends, contributed in such meaningful ways. Each time the work faced a pause, one of you stepped in and gave it a push. I so value your insights, your encouragement, and especially the greater joy of sharing life's adventures with you and your families.

To Patrick, who has never stopped encouraging me to "write the book," gifting journals, writing tools, and even a three-day retreat to help make it happen. You believed in this long before the manuscript existed—and kept nudging, cheering, and reminding me to keep going. No one dreams bigger than you…a Seven Roles theme park?!

To Kevan, who created the first Seven Roles seminar years ago for his workplace, bridging the gap between personal insight and professional application. Your original slides showed me how naturally the roles could support leadership and strengthen teams. That shift changed everything. I stopped thinking one-on-one and started thinking bigger. And now look where we are.

To Erin, who built a successful and amazing business around teaching and applying the Seven Roles, proving their measurable impact on individuals, teams, and organizations. From my scribbled notes, you shaped classes that are engaging, well-constructed, and frequently, life changing. You create an environment where people don't just understand the roles—they *enjoy* them. You make 'role growth' feel possible. More importantly, you make real growth feel possible.

To Meaghan, whose support throughout the journey of this book, and the roles company, has been invaluable. You engaged with every part of the research, from statistical models to practical applications, offering encouragement, information and improvements. Your ability to balance analytical precision with a deep care for people is your greatest strength; not only with the roles, but in life.

To **Kevin Woods**, whose creative thinking and technical expertise turned a problem I couldn't solve into a platform I could build on. Your thoughtful questioning helped shape both the foundation and the framework where the Seven Team Roles Scale (STRS) exists today. Your work building and maintaining MyTeamRole made it possible for the roles to reach far beyond my desk—and into the lives of others.

To my **family and friends who are like family**—your meaningful contributions, thoughtful discussions, and encouragement have shaped this book in ways both big and small. I've even borrowed your names and sprinkled them across the examples in these pages—a testament to the impact you've had on this journey. I am so grateful for each of you.

To **Dr. Corene Poelman-Stewart**, for your meticulous proofreading of every version and unwavering encouragement. You and **Bryan** took version one of the scale nearly a decade ago—on paper. Remember that?

To **Pam Bretz**, for your enthusiastic reading of the final draft and for liking it enough to want to share it. And for the courage to *face* the next steps when I needed it most.

To **Jamie Duke and Chrissy Levas**, for taking all the initial scales, providing helpful insights, and—most importantly—supplying the most important ingredient: abundant joy.

To **Judy and Tim Smith**, for being great 'role' models. You exemplify all the roles as you build your big outrageous life dream.

To **Quinlan and Madeleine Smith**, for your creative work on the unique Seven Roles logo and your directing and video expertise.

To **Eric Komosa**, for your keen editorial eye and the many cups of coffee that fueled this process—first editing the dissertation and then each of the book versions.

To **all who have explored the Seven Roles** over the years, whether in conversation, workshops, or through the scale, your feedback, application and enthusiasm have refined this work. Thank you for allowing me to witness the Seven Roles in action in so many different lives. **Ariana Papa,** this includes you.

Thank you all for your limitless support of my seemingly limitless enthusiasm for the Seven Roles.

Finally, to **you, the reader**—this journey is now yours. My hope is that you are stretched in the best and most helpful ways to **be more… you**.

> *'The best part of life is who you get to share it with."*

ABOUT THE AUTHOR

Dr. Nancy McConlogue is the innovator of the Seven Roles framework, developed over three decades of professional practice, personal experience and research. Her passion for understanding and guiding human behavior led her to validate the framework inspired by Romans 12.

Dr. Nancy earned her degree in computer science from UCSD (1983), followed by a master's in counseling (2001) and doctorate in IO psychology from SCS (2018). She has applied the Seven Roles in therapy, teaching, and coaching settings, helping countless individuals unlock their potential by practicing meaningful change.

She and her husband, Sean, recently celebrated their 40th anniversary. They have four children, now adults with beautiful families of their own.

When not writing, coaching, reading or teaching, Dr. Nancy enjoys spending time with her family and friends, leaning into her Team Builder Role which is her favorite.

For more information about the Seven Roles, visit: SevenRoles.com

Made in the USA
Columbia, SC
17 July 2025